IMITATING CHRIST

Religious Experience Series

Edward J. Malatesta, S.J., General Editor

Volumes in Preparation:
Paths to Contemplation
Contemplation in the Greek Fathers
The Theology of Contemplation

Religious Experience Series

Volume 5

Imitating Christ

by
Edouard Cothenet, Canon Etienne Ledeur, Pierre Adnés,
Aimé Solignac, S.J., Bernard Spaapen, S.J.

Translated by
Sister Simone Inkel, S.L.
and
Sister Lucy Tinsley, S.N.D.

With a Preface by
John L. Boyle, S.J.

ABBEY PRESS
St. Meinrad, Indiana 47577
1974

The present work is a translation of the article "Imitation du Christ" and of the second part of the article "Imitation du Christ (Livre)" which first appeared in the *Dictionnaire de Spiritualité,* Paris, Beauchesne, 1971, vol. 7, Deuxième partie, cols. 1536-1601 and 2355-2368 respectively.

© 1974 by Edward Malatesta, S.J.
Library of Congress Catalog Card Number: 73-94173
ISBN: 0-87029-029-0
Printed in the United States of America

Preface

John L. Boyle, S.J.

For nearly two thousand years, Christians have confessed Jesus of Nazareth to be the Christ, Son of God, and risen Lord. Object of faith and center of worship, Jesus has also captured the imaginations and inspired the religious ideals of His followers who have sought to pattern their own lives on that of their Master. The sources and historical development of this ideal—the imitation of Christ—form the theme of this volume in the new Religious Experience Series.

The present translation makes available for English readers a collection of five brief articles from the *Dictionnaire de Spiritualité,* each dealing in a different way with this theme. Examining the ideal of the imitation of Christ in the Synoptic Gospels, the Letters of Paul, some other Epistles, and, finally, the Gospel of John, the first chapter focuses on that source which for centuries has nourished the piety of Christians. The second chapter briefly sketches the development of this ideal in the lives and writings of the saints down to our present time. The third and fourth chapters examine the theology and pastoral aspects of this theme; and the final chapter serves as a *vade mecum* to the classic: *The Imitation of Christ.*

Imitation of the virtues of the gods was an ethical ideal for the Greeks. The Hebrews were more conscious both of God's transcendence and of His active presence in the history of His chosen people. For them, the religious and moral demand of their calling was "to follow in the way(s) of the Lord," to obey His precepts, to hear His word. This language of "following the way" was a natural expression for the adherence of the dis-

ciples to Jesus during His ministry in Palestine. More than
mere observance of precepts, it also implied a community of
life (at that time, the normal relationship of disciple to teacher). But the formulation of the relation between Jesus and
His disciples in the Gospels does more than describe the manner of life of Jesus and his followers years ago in Palestine.
The description of the call of the first disciples is meant to be
the paradigm of the vocation of every Christian. And His
"Way" par excellence is the total giving of Himself which
climaxed in His death and resurrection. The inner unity between the destiny of Jesus and that of His disciples emerges
from the close relationship Jesus makes between His own impending Passion and the conditions for discipleship (see Mk
8:31-38). "Following" Jesus, then, does not mean merely
obeying His commands or patterning one's external actions on
His, but living out the basic interior attitude of His life in
union with Him.

Paul never knew Jesus "according to the flesh." He became
a disciple of the risen Lord. And so, Paul does not use the
language of "following," which better fits the pre-Paschal period, but that of "imitation." But he focuses more intently on
the inner attitude of Jesus, His self-giving, as well as on the personal union in faith and sacrament between the Christian and
Christ. "Have this mind in you which is in Christ Jesus" (Phil
2:5). And since the power of the Gospel is communicated by
living as well as by preaching, Paul is not reluctant to encourage
the Churches which knew him to imitate him, Paul, as he imitates Jesus (1 Cor 11:1).

The organic unity between the inner life of Jesus with His
Father and this inner life as source of the life of the Christian
is most forcefully expressed in word and symbol in the Gospel
of John. St. John gives most emphasis to the depth of personal
intimacy between the believer and Jesus and the fruit of this
in the giving of self to others in the community.

The description of the martyrdom of Stephen in the Acts
of the Apostles is a clear example of a Christian whose death
is an "imitation" of the death of Jesus precisely because his
inner attitude is joined to and flows from the inner life of his
risen Lord. It was only natural that the writings of the first
Fathers would present the martyrs as the ideal of the imitation

of Christ. As the historical expression of Jesus' complete self-giving was His death on the Cross, so, too, the perfect imitation of Christ was the death of the martyrs.

The sermons of the Fathers instinctively appeal more to the example and inner dispositions of Christ as the rule of Christian life than to external precepts. St. John Chrysostom when speaking on the Eucharist emphasizes the dispositions of the Christian who is nourished by the Eucharist more than he does the Sacrament itself. For St. Bernard, the imitation of Christ becomes a touchstone of faith: "When finally I believed in Christ, that is to say when I imitated His humility, I came to know Truth." And the emphasis on the interior life by the spiritual writers of the 17th and 18th centuries was motivated by the same desire for genuine faith as that of Paul and the Fathers.

But the lives of the saints even more than their writings give compelling evidence to the place of the imitation of Christ in the life of the Church. St. Francis of Assisi and Charles de Foucauld were two of many whose lives were inspired by this ideal. And if some of their actions seem to be a too literalistic interpretation of the teachings of Christ, their motivation was not merely an attempt to comply with an external norm but to live out an interior attachment. Their lives ring true.

Perhaps it is this quality of genuine piety which shines through the pages of the *Imitation of Christ* and has influenced the lives of so many. It is clear that the author had meditated long on the Bible and that he strove to cultivate a deep interior life. He has sometimes been accused of being anti-social; but this same impression might be given in parts of *Markings* by Dag Hammarskjöld, who was hardly a hermit. The author was a man of his time and this conditioned both his style and approach. But his emphasis on the interior life as the key to a true imitation of Christ has much to offer even today.

Psychologists and sociologists emphasize the crucial importance of imitation in the development of both individual and social life. Education, in its most effective sense, rests on imitation. Moral growth, in particular, takes place when the values incarnated in an ideal person are so present to the individual or group that the traits of that person are incorporated into oneself. And often the influence is more powerful when the individual is less aware of being shaped by the model.

The experience of this formative action within the individual is that of an attraction; he experiences that the originating force of his own action is no longer within himself. As this experience develops and becomes more precise, the attraction becomes love. Scheler says: "It is in the radiant beauty of real presons, in the example which shapes our very lives that we must first of all find the origin and stimulus for moral progress and not primarily in the formal rules of universal acceptance. What operates within us is a modification or, more precisely, a conversion of the condition of our spirit under the influence of the model-person. The ideal does not decide our actions, but we become imbued with the spirit of the model. In this way we learn to desire and to act in the manner in which the model desires and acts, but not desire what he desires, nor do what he does."

The imitation of Christ is much more profound but not less human. Christian faith is adherence to a person. And so a personalist ethic can be applied to Christianity. But Jesus can not be recognized and adhered to as He is, the Son of God, without the gift of faith. The attraction to Jesus for what He is, is the work of God. "No one can come to me unless the Father who sent me draws him" (Jn 6:44). To recognize Jesus is to recognize that God shares His own life with man out of love. "God so loved the world that He gave His own Son" (Jn 3:16). At the same time, faith recognizes that God communicates and wishes to communicate His life to me. This recognition of faith implies at its deepest level an awareness of being recognized by God (1 Cor 13:12).

The chief characteristics of the imitation of Christ flow from the incarnational mode of God's communicating His life to us. It is fundamentally *sacramental* since Christ is the fundamental sacrament of God's encounter with man. It is *ecclesial* since it is primarily through the Church that we come to know Christ. And it is principally the work of the *Holy Spirit,* the Spirit of Christ: "It is no longer I who live but Christ who lives in me" (Gal 2:20).

The natural means of imitating Christ in Christian piety has always been an affective contemplation of the Gospels.

Since the Gospels describe not merely past events but present mysteries, this contemplation is not an attempt to recapture the past but to sink one's roots more deeply into the ground of Christian existence. But for such imitation to be actively lived in the present, the Christian must grow in sensitivity to the needs of others and openness to the aspirations of man today. This particular aspect of the imitation of Christ is perhaps not emphasized enough here but not everything can be said in a brief book.

The chapters of this book were originally brief articles from an Encyclopedia. As such they present an overview of a theme that has a long and colorful history. It is hoped that an interest in one or another aspect of the Imitation of Christ will lead the reader to take advantage of the rich bibliography given in the notes to each chapter.

More than for better theological formulations, syntheses, or insights, contemporary Christians feel a need for a deeper, more personal religious experience. And the world needs more saints. A genuine imitation of Christ can serve both needs. This book is offered with that in mind.

A special thanks to Sisters Simone Inkel and Lucy Tinsley, translators of chapters one to four and of chapter five respectively, and to Fr. Felix Donahue, monk of Our Lady of Gethsemani, who helped prepare the notes. Their patient and accurate work has made it possible to share with many these articles from the prestigious *Dictionnaire de Spiritualité*.

John L. Boyle, S.J
Berkeley, California

List of Abbreviations

ACW	Ancient Christian Writers	Westminster, Md.
ANF	Ante-Nicene Fathers	Grand Rapids (reprint)
CF	Cistercian Fathers	Washington, D.C.
DS	*Dictionnaire de Spiritualité*	Paris
FC	Fathers of the Church	New York; Washington, D.C.
FT	French translation	
NPNF	Nicene and Post-Nicene Fathers	Grand Rapids (reprint)
RAM	*Revue d'ascétique et de mystique*	Toulouse
RES	Religious Experience Series	St. Meinrad, Ind.
TDNT	Theological Dictionary of the New Testament	Grand Rapids

Contents

Chapter I

Sacred Scripture

by Edouard Cothenet

In the history of spirituality the theme of the imitation of Christ holds an important place. Although the verb "to imitate" is not found in the gospels, Christians understood that the invitation to "follow" Jesus was a call to imitate him. As St. Augustine wrote, "for, what is it to follow Him except to imitate Him?"[1] This was the accepted interpretation until the time of the Reformation. Then came a time of change: while recognizing that Christ is both Gift and Example, Luther began increasingly to accentuate the aspect of Gift. Reacting against medieval piety, he tended to see in this imitation of Christ a possible pride-filled tendency on the part of man to acquire merit on his own. The Reformation remained marked by this suspicion. To the imitation of Christ *(Nachahmung),* it opposed the following of Christ *(Nachfolge)* as a response in faith and obedience to the call of Christ.

Luther's critique contains some truth. One cannot imitate Christ as one would a human hero. To use the words of J. Guitton, "if Jesus is a man, He is only a model, a hero . . . But if He is God, what there exists in common between Him and His followers is something of a wholly different order, to be identified only as the relationship between the Uncreated and human minds."[2] And when, attracted by the personality of Christ, one attempts to reproduce His style of life, it must never be forgotten that it is Christ Himself who draws us towards this imitation. The effort of the believer to "put on" his Master emerges out of the world of grace and not out of stoic determination.

The theme of imitation holds very little place in the *Concordance* of the Bible. *The Vocabulary of Biblical Theology* does not even have an article on *Imitation* and refers the reader to the words "Disciple" and "Follow." In this instance, the philological inquiry is deceptive; it is well known that there is not an exact correspondence in the meaning of words from one language to another and that one must take care to grasp the idea far more than the words. For this reason, we will retain a number of texts in which the vocabulary of imitation does not appear but in which the idea is clearly implied.

A. The Old Testament

In contrast to the Greek world in which imitation is held in high regard either in philosophical reflection (Plato), or in its conception of art as an imitation of nature (Plato and Aristotle), or in its pedagogy (the attractive value of example), the Bible seems to ignore the virtues of imitation. The Septuagint hardly uses the words *mimeomai* and *mimētēs* ("imitation" and "imitator").

In reality, this concept finds expression at another level. Israel lives in a universe of "solidarity"; in a community which has a common destiny; the father and his descendants are so united that the life of the ancestors determines the destiny of the tribe or the nation.[3] It is presumed that the sons will follow the ways of their fathers.

An example of this is the typical response of the Rechabites when Jeremiah offers them a cup of wine: "We will drink no wine, for Jonadab the son of Rechab, our Father, commanded us: You shall not drink wine, neither you nor your sons forever; you shall not build a house; you shall not sow seed; you shall not plant or have a vineyard; but you shall live in tents all your days, that you may live many days in the land where you sojourn" (Jer 35:6-7). Jeremiah uses this example of fidelity to stigmatize the conduct of his contemporaries who have abandoned the God of their fathers in order to follow strange gods.

In contrast to the Greeks, the Israelites do not express their understanding of life in abstract terms, but in terms that are concrete. As ancient nomads, they use freely the theme of the way *(derek)* and of journey *(halak aharay,* to walk behind; *halak be,* to walk in, understood as conducting oneself in such and such a way). Like the Egyptians, their books of wisdom are the instructions of a father to his son. While the Greek sage addresses himself as a friend to his disciples, the Oriental claims paternal authority and considers his disciples as sons (e.g. Prov 1:8; 2:1; 3:1; etc.). They are to "walk in the way of their father." It is within this context that we find the concept of imitation, since instruction is not divorced from the reality of life.[4] That is why Paul invites the faithful to imitate him because he has become their father in Christ Jesus through the gospel (1 Cor 4:16).

The later books of the Bible offer the example given by the ancients for emulation. And so Judith (8:21-23) recalls the way Isaac, Jacob and Moses pleased God in an hour of trial. Ben Sirach (44-50) presents a magnificent array of the ancients to his disciples in order to invite them to resist the attraction of Greek ways and persevere in the ways of the Fathers.[5] In this same style, the author of Hebrews (chap. 11) enumerates a list of witnesses who have been splendid examples of faith for us.

The difference in mentality between the biblical world and the Greek world again appears clearly in the understanding of the imitation of God. The stoic philosophers in particular assign to man the task of imitating the perfections of the gods:

"The man who wants to please and obey the gods must strive to realize the greatest possible resemblance with them. If the deity is faithful, he must be faithful; if free, he too, must be free; if kind, he too must be kind; if generous, he too must be generous. Henceforth, he must both speak and act as one who emulates God."[6] Philo of Alexandria is inspired by such thoughts when he bases our obligation to resemble God on the fact that we are created to His image and likeness.[7]

Although this principle is found in Genesis, we cannot say that the Old Testament develops the idea of the imitation of God; the emphasis is placed on the divine transcendence and fidelity to the covenant. The demand of the Code of Holiness, "You shall be holy; for I the Lord your God am holy" (Lv 19:2), certainly does not mean that man can imitate the divine holiness. Because God's Being is wholly Other, beyond all possible representation (that is why images of God are forbidden, Ex 20:4), the people of Israel, and each of its members, must abstain not only from all imperfection but also from all impurity (in the ritual sense). The constant refrain is that man must "walk in the ways of the Lord"; in this sense we can speak of "walking behind the Lord." "You shall walk after the Lord your God and fear Him, and keep His commandments and obey His voice, and you shall serve Him and cleave to Him" (Dt 13:4).

In this verse, the accumulation of synonyms highlights the various aspects of the theme of following the Lord (see also 1 Kgs 14:8; 18:21; 2 Kgs 23:3). The notion of obedience is dominant, an obedience which in Deuteronomy is ennobled by love (Dt 5:33; 6:5 etc.). However, the Torah, and not God in His supreme majesty, is the norm according to which a man must regulate his conduct.

A few rabbinical texts written after New Testament times express an invitation to imitate the mercy of God. Thus Abba Saul declared: "I will resemble Him (God); just as He is merciful and compassionate, so shall I be merciful and compassionate." "The Holy One, may He be blessed, is called merciful: be equally merciful; He is also called compassionate: be you likewise compassionate . . . He is called full of goodness: be you also full of goodness."

B. *The Following of Christ in the Synoptic Gospels*

In contrast to the remainder of the New Testament, the gospels (the Synoptics and John) constantly use the verb *akolouthein,* (to follow), to designate the attachment of the disciples to Jesus. To follow after Jesus seems to be the characteristic attitude of those whom He has called and who are preeminently the witnesses to His actions and His teaching. But in the gospels, the vocabulary of imitation is lacking, although it is certainly present in the Pauline *corpus.* This difference of language draws attention to a more profound difference: the relationship of the disciples with Jesus cannot be the same kind as that of those believers, for example, Paul, who never knew the Jesus of history and yet lived by faith in the glorified *Kyrios.* The distinction between the *Nachfolge,* which marks

the pre-paschal times, and the *Nachahmung,* which character-
izes the times that followed, is therefore necessary. It is advisable then to ask ourselves whether, in the gospel *following*
of Jesus, the essential dispositions are already present which will
evolve into the *imitation* of Jesus in the Pauline sense.

Methodological reflections. The bibliography is extensive.
We will limit ourselves to pointing out the most outstanding
contributions made in the last decade.

a) Catholic studies. The principle work is that of Anselm
Shulz, *Nachfolgen und Nachahmen, Studien über das Verhält-
nis der neutestamentlichen Jüngershaft zur unchristlichen Vor-
bildthik* (Munich, 1962); summarized in *Junger des Herrn*
(Munich, 1964); FT: *Suivre et imiter le Christ d'après le nouveau Testament* (Paris, 1966), referred to here. Schulz is greatly influenced by the articles in Kittel: *"Akoloutheō,"* by G. Kittel, TDNT, vol. 1, pp. 210-216; *"Mimeomai, etc."* by W. Michaelis, TDNT, vol. 4, pp. 659-674. He uses the method of
Formgeschichte and, without sufficient awareness of the hypothetical character of his classification, he opposes to systematically the various layers of tradition. According to him, *akolouthein* (follow) has six different meanings: physical accompaniment by the people, the sympathizers, the Twelve or a few isolated disciples; the obligation of the pupil (Lk 14:27; Mk 8:34);
the metaphor of the *mathētēs* (disciple) (Mk 1:17-18; Mt 19:
28); sharing a common destiny (Jn 12:26; 13:36-37; Rev 14:
4); a derived meaning: to believe (Jn 8:12; 10:4-5 and 27); a
moral connotation: to follow=to imitate (Lk 14:27; Mk 8:34;
1 Pt 2:21). Schulz insists greatly on a correspondence between
the relationship of Jesus with His disciples and the relationship
of a Jewish master and his pupils (pp. 13-24). This point of
view has been rejected by K. H. Rengstorf, in his article *Man-
thano* in TDNT, vol. 4, especially pp. 434-461, *passim.* Schulz
fails to stress adequately the community life which existed between Jesus and His disciples.

R. Schnackenburg gives an accurate overview of the texts
in *The Moral Teaching of the New Testament* (Freiburg,
1965), pp. 42-43, 161-167, 207-217.

We find in C. Spicq's *Théologie morale du nouveau Testament* a wealth of references and valuable insights (pp. 688-
744). All references are classified around the theme of the

image of God which is normal from a systematic point of view, but such a classification does not allow for a sense of historical development of the theme of the imitation of Christ.

b) Protestant studies. E. Larsson's *Christus als Vorbild: Eine Untersuchung zu den paulinischen Tauf—und Eikontexten* (Upsala, 1962) concentrates on an interpretation of the texts which put baptism in relationship to the death and resurrection of Christ (Rom 6:1-11; Col 2:11, 3:4; Gal 2:19-20; Eph 2:4-7), and on those which consider Christ as the image of God (Col 3:10 ff. [and 1:15]; Eph 4:24; Phil 2:5-11; 2 Cor 3:18 and 4:4; Rom 8:28-30; 1 Cor 15:44-49). The author has been careful to link the teaching of St. Paul with the gospel tradition. A chapter to which we are much indebted is that on *Nachfolge Jesu* ("following Jesus") in the gospels (pp. 29-47).

c) In 1966, the *Ephemerides theologicae lovanienses* published two important contributions by Thysman and by Aerts. R. Thysman studies *L'éthique de l'imitation du Christ dans le nouveau Testament. Situations, notations et variations du thème* (42 [1966] 138-175). The author clearly distinguishes the theological theme of "following Christ," which is essentially religious, and the theme of imitation, which is ethical. In the case of "following Christ" or "being a disciple," "it is a matter of a stable community or a communion of life in Christ which, because of the divine initiative, is gift, is grace." The ethical concept of *imitation,* seldom found in the Synoptic gospels but developed in the epistles, appears primarily within the context of parenesis or of baptismal liturgy (p. 147). In spite of the occasionally artificial nature of this distinction, R. Thysman has drafted a good chapter of biblical theology and concludes by stressing the importance of the imitation of Christ in moral theology.

Th. Aerts (*Suivre Jésus. Evolution d'un thème biblique dans les évangiles synoptiques,* pp. 476-512, with a rich bibliography) thinks that although modern critics insist on the unique perspective of each evangelist *(Traditionsgeschichte)* the theme of "to follow Jesus" can be studied in the three Synoptics together. He distinguishes three stages: 1) the tradition of the pre-community period (centered on the call of the disciples); 2) the tradition of the community period (the conditions for the following of Jesus); 3) the tradition of the redactional period. The distinction between the first and second periods often remains hypothetical. But in general one can appreciate the refined analyses of Th. Aerts, who knows how to distance himself from the systematic positions of the German critics.

d) In 1967-1968 there appeared in German two Protestant studies which were in a way diametrically opposed to each other. In *Nachfolge und Nachahmung Jesus Christi im Neuen Testament* (Tübingen, 1967), H. D. Betz attempts to distinguish between the *Nachfolge,* a Palestinian concept, and the cultic *Mimesis* found in the mystery religions. In the first part we are told that it is hardly possible to know what really was the relationship between Jesus and His disciples. Betz ascribes to the *Gemeindetheologie* ("the theology elaborated by the community") most of the *logia* ("sayings of Jesus") related to the following of Jesus. The structure of Paul is not gnostic but is related to the mystery cults *(Mysterienhaft).* Paul knew nothing of the historical Jesus (p. 178) and for him it is simply a matter of the configuration of the Christian to the death and resurrection of Christ. The theme of moral imitation does not appear until 1 Peter and finds its culmination in the *Martyrdom of Polycarp.*

The thesis of M. Hengel, *Nachfolge und Charisma. Eine exegetischreligionsgeschichtliche Studie zu Mt. 8:21f. und Jesu Ruf in die Nachfolge* (Berlin, 1968), is a lively reaction against the idea that Jesus related to His disciples as a rabbi. Using the *logion* "Follow me and let the dead bury their dead," he puts emphasis on the prophetic and eschatological character of this call and compares it to that of the Zealot "prophets," who were then numerous and sought to lure the people into the desert to receive the "signs of salvation." We might add that M. Hengel clearly emphasizes the difference between Jesus and the Zealots. One can appreciate in this work the effort to discover the Jesus of history beyond all the contestable hypotheses which are related to the *Gemeindetheologie,* but one must guard against seeing Jesus only as one who proclaims an imminent eschatological crisis.

1. The Imitation of God in the Preaching of Jesus

Mark summarizes the first preaching of Jesus in these few words: "The time is fulfilled, and the kingdom of God is at

hand; repent, and believe in the gospel" (1:15). It is an eschatological proclamation which cannot be understood unless we
put it within the context of a period that was marked by an
ardent expectation of the end times (see the apocalypses and the
Qumran texts) and especially by John the Baptist's radical call.
The turning point of history has arrived. God takes His cause
in hand and establishes His Kingdom among men. Men are
called to enter into this event by means of a complete change
of heart *(metanoia)*.[8]

Jesus does not restrict Himself to declaring that the promises
of Scripture are about to be fulfilled (Lk 4:18-19); He presents Himself as the one through whom the Good News accomplishes its work, according to the traditional understanding
of God's efficacious Word (Is 55:10-11, and the parable of
the sower). At the same time He tries to help His hearers to
discover the true nature of God's kingdom, which they imagine
in forms that are too external and too often marked by national-
ism. Many authors present Jesus in too simplistic a way as one
who announces the End *(Naherwartung)*. J. Ratzinger says that
from a historical point of view such a watering down of the
message of Jesus makes the development of Christianity incom-
prehensible.[9] If Jesus is just an apocalyptic figure among many
others of that time, why would His work have survived?

In reality, in the announcing of the Kingdom the manifestation of God's Name has an essential place. Because Jesus Himself lives as Son in a unique way, He says *Abba!* with an intensity that profoundly impresses those who hear Him. By
His words and actions, He reveals the true face of God and
teaches His disciple to glorify the Father who sees in secret.
He inculcates a sense of their dignity as men not by saying
they are created in God's image but by existentially teaching
them to live in God's presence and to call Him Father.

Jesus teaches us to aspire to the very perfection of God
(according to Mt 5:48). The parallel text in Luke, which har-
monizes better with the previous context (love of one's enemies)
and seems in greater conformity to the original saying of Jesus,
invites us to be merciful: "Become (*ginesthe;* there is an effort
to be sustained) merciful, even as your Father is merciful" (Lk
6:36). In this way men will be "sons of the Most High" (v.
35).[10]

The mercy of the Father, who lets His sun shine and His rain fall on the just and on sinners, is in reality made flesh through the ministry of Jesus who, to the scandal of the Pharisees, welcomes public sinners and eats at their table. A good example of this is the way Jesus, when narrating His parables of mercy (Lk 15), justifies His conduct by referring to the way His Father acts.

The imitation of God for a Christian then is not primarily the pursuit of an abstract perfection as conceived by philosophical reflection, but an imitation of God which involves our history and is revealed to us in Jesus Christ.[11]

We will see, in the only Pauline passage in which there is a question of *imitation of God* (Eph 5:1), that this passage is intimately related to mutual forgiveness (4:32) and the example of Christ (5:2). There is a striking correspondence between the doctrine of Paul and that of Luke which permits us to conclude that Paul in this instance is referring to an evangelical tradition.

2. The Call of the Disciples

The most distinctive use of the verb *akolouthein* (follow) in the Synoptic gospels is found in the vocation narratives: the call of the first four apostles on the shore of the lake of Galilee (Mk 1:16-20 ff.), the call of Levi at his tax-collector's desk (2:13-14 ff.), and of various groups within the perspectives of the messianic signs of Jesus (Mt 8:18-22) or in the passage of the journey to Jerusalem (Lk 9:57-62).

This literary genre is appraised in various ways. M. Dibelius is without doubt right in seeing in it paradigms structured for parenetical purposes.[12] The story is told in order to create an openness to the Lord's call. There is no truly analogous structure between the vocation of the apostles in Mark and the vocation of Elijah (1 Kgs 19:19-21). Even more than the author of the Book of Kings who writes a true story, the evangelist centers everything on the word of Jesus: "Follow me and I will make you become fishers of men" (Mk 1:17). In his commentary E. Lohmeyer compares the decisive call of Jesus to the efficacious Word of God as it operates in the vocation of the great prophets of the Old Testament.[13] There is no indication of interest in the psychological attitude of those called;

only the Word of Christ matters and the assiduous obedience of the disciple.

"To follow the Master," says A. Schulz, "expressed the relationship of the disciple to his Master."[14] Analogies between Jesus' way of acting and that of the rabbis are certainly not lacking. Although Jesus never frequented the schools (see Jn 7:15), He gives evidence of a knowledge of Scripture which enables Him to disarm His adversaries in discussions. Typical of His day, He uses sayings in which each word has its counterpart in a second saying; He uses techniques of composition which facilitate memorization; and He creates numerous parables. After having taught the crowds, He takes his disciples apart to explain to them what they did not understand and reserves for them the revelation of "the mysteries of the Kingdom." These analogies, studied thoroughly by B. Gerhardsson,[15] offer the greatest interest for a study of the transmission of the gospel tradition, but they do not enable us to recognize the unique character of the relationship which Jesus establishes with those whom He called to Himself.

It has been shown, for example, by K. H. Rengstorf[16] and M. Hengel[17] that Jesus' action does not have a standard common with that of the doctors of the law. Ordinarily, young men who desire to know the Torah seek a master and study under him, not in order to follow him personally but in order to study the Torah.[18] The more disciples a master has, the more he is honored. A student remains at the feet of his master as long as he has not learned all that the master has to teach him. From that point on he becomes an independent master. The gospel situation is totally different. The vocation scenes are centered on one's attachment to the person of Jesus, who takes the initiative and acts with an authority that is prophetic.

3. Following Jesus and Sharing Life in Common

Sensitive to the bond between the call of Jesus and being sent on mission, A. Schulz concludes that "in the most ancient strata of the Synoptic tradition, the expression 'to follow Jesus' simply implies a function, a service, that of the liberation of the entire people of Israel" and that the hard demands made by Jesus are only "the professional conditions."[19]

There are certain reservations to express regarding this particular interpretation. It is true that Jesus calls His disciples to associate them with His work of preaching and casting out of demons (compare Mt 10:1,7 and 4:23-25), but the use of the word "professional" risks leading into error. In our modern world, frequently the most personal and most dynamic kind of action happens within the context of a complementary action which is freely chosen in a spirit of total gratuity. What we find in the gospel is that the function of the disciple bound to the proclamation of the Kingdom operates within the context of a life shared in common with the Master. The narrative of the appointment of the Twelve by Mark is quite revealing: "Jesus appointed twelve to be with Him and to be sent out to preach" (3:14). Life shared in common and being sent on mission are linked indissolubly: the mission can be fulfilled only if this "being with Jesus" enables the apostle to be truly a representative of His Master.

The rabbi of the past had nothing in common with the modern professor who establishes a distinction between his teaching and his private life. The rabbi formed his disciples not only by his interpretation of the Torah, but also by the way he practiced it in his daily life.[20] This kind of formation is affirmed throughout the gospels. If Jesus called fishermen from the lake to Himself, He shared with them His very life. As soon as He went aside to pray, the disciples immediately began to look for Him (Mk 1:35-36 ff.). Far from presenting Christ as a Master who dictated unreal sayings, the gospel gives evidence that He took concrete situations as a point of departure for His teachings: discussions on the traditions of the ancients, the questions of the disciples, reprehensible attitudes that needed correction, etc. It is in such a life shared in common that Jesus formed His own for their future mission. Did not His example play an important role?

Traditionally, the rabbis expected their disciples to serve them.[21] It is quite different with Jesus. If He forms His apostles for action and asks their help for the ministry, He never adopts the attitude of a leader who uses for His own profit the availability of others. Jesus calls attention to the paradoxical character of His way of acting: "I am among you as one who serves" (Lk 22:27). This same attitude He bequeaths as an obligation for those who will follow Him: "The kings of the

Gentiles exercise lordship over them; and those in authority over them are called benefactors. But not so with you; rather let the greatest among you become as the youngest, and the leader as one who serves" (22:25-26). *To be with* Jesus is to discover a kind of greatness which is different from that of flesh or of intelligence; it is to enter into the realm of a unique kind of love which Jesus came to reveal.

The narrative of the vocation of the apostles is marked by a demand for detachment from one's family and possessions.[22] We will select a particularly dramatic example. "One of His disciples said to him, 'Lord, let me first go and bury my father.' But Jesus said to him, 'Follow me *(akolouthei moi)* and leave the dead to bury their own dead'" (Mt 7:21-22 and Lk 9:59-60). In the ancient world there was nothing more sacred than the duty of burying the dead. The decision of Jesus breaks with the law and customs of the time and has no precedent except for Jeremiah who was forbidden to take part in funerals (Jer 16:5-7) or Ezechiel who was forbidden to mourn for his wife (Ez 24:16-17). But in both of these cases, the divine command signified the impending terrible catastrophe to which no individual sorrow could possibly compare. The emphasis of the word of Jesus is very different. It is not the somber announcement of an imminent Judgment, but it is one which creates peace: "Go in peace; your faith has saved you" (Lk 5:48 etc). It is important to note the price required for union with the One who restores Life.

In order to understand these strong demands we must see how Jesus Himself lived them out in a radical kind of detachment. To the scribe who decided to follow Him wherever He went, the Master answered: "Foxes have holes, and birds of the air have nests; but the Son of man has nowhere to lay His head" (Mt 8:20). In almost brutal terms, Mark remembers this demand of separation from one's family. "And his friends went out to seize Him, for they said: He is besides Himself *(exestē)*" (Mk 3:21). To those who called His attention to the presence of His mother and His brothers and sisters, Jesus replied: "Here are my mother and my brothers! Whoever does the will of God is my brother, and sister and mother" (Mk 3:34-35). It is a new kind of family which Jesus establishes around Himself by revealing the will of His Father.

4. Following Jesus and Carrying the Cross

In the life of Jesus, His question to the apostles and the confession of Peter at Caesarea Philippi mark a decisive turning point. Immediately following this scene, Jesus "began to teach them that the Son of man must suffer many things, and be rejected by the elders and the chief priests and the scribes, and be killed, and after three days rise again" (Mk 8:31-33). This teaching seemed such a scandal to Peter that he felt obliged to bring his Master back to a sense of His messianic mission. But he only received the sharp response that is reminiscent of Christ's response to the Tempter (Mt 4:10 par.). In his desire to turn his Master away from the cross and keep Him within the perspectives of a popular messianism, Peter played the part of Satan. If he wants to remain a "disciple," he must renounce all hopes that are too human. Does not "behind me" contain a reminder of the demands of one's vocation? "A disciple is not above his master" (Mt 10:24); it is not for him to mitigate the demands of His teaching.

This severe admonition is followed by an invitation to carry the cross: "If any man would come after me, let him deny himself and take up his cross and follow me" (Mk 8:34 par.; this *logion* is found in other contexts: Mt 10:38 and Lk 14:27). The opening redactional statement varies from one evangelist to the other. Matthew, who preserves the most ancient text, only mentions the "disciples"; Mark and Luke broaden the audience to show that this scene applies to all Christians.

Some critics have rejected the authenticity of this call by arguing that Jesus could not foresee His own death and *a fortiori* that of His disciples. E. Dinkler tried to rediscover the primitive meaning: it is not a question of the cross but of the Sign of one's belonging to God (represented by the letter *tau,* which has the shape of a cross according to Ez 9:4-5).[23] Such an explanation rests on an hypothesis that creates more difficulties than it solves!

Contrary to critics who see these texts as creations of the Christian community after Easter, J. Jeremias has shown the archaic character of the Passion predictions in the gospels and relates them to the prophecies of the Servant of Yahweh which are so prominent in the message of Jesus.[24]

On the other hand, as was recently pointed out by M. Hengel[25] and J. Gwyn Griffiths,[26] punishment by crucifixion on a cross was not rare in Palestine during the first century, which was often disturbed by "Zealot prophets" who called followers in order to use them to liberate the country.

This comparison does not mean that Jesus shared the ideals of the Zealots; He could, by using a quasi-proverbial expression, show that in order for His disciples to enter Life, they must be ready to confront the severest trials.

Despite a few variations, the general development of the theme of renouncing oneself and losing one's life for Christ in the Synoptic gospels are sufficiently similar and sufficiently related to the preceding passage to enable us to go back to a pre-Synoptic level of tradition. The relatedness of the ideas is best perceived by the repetition of a key word, *opisō mou* (after me). Following N. A. Dahl,[27] Th. Aerts[28] compares this structure with the one found in Rom 15:2-3 and 7-8; Mk 10:44-45; I Pt 2:21-24; 3:18-20; and in Phil 2:5-7. This observation indicates that very early the theme of the *imitation of Christ (imitatio Christi)* was linked with that of *following Christ (sequela Christi).*

Is the concept that the disciple must participate in the fate of his Master to be found only at the community level of the text or can we situate it at an even earlier level? Before Easter the words of Christ could not possibly have had the clarity they would acquire later on. The gospel tells us that the prediction of the Passion was a language beyond the understanding of the disciples. In spite of these reservations, can we not ask if these words of Jesus do not contain in principle the doctrine which would later be made explicit by the Christian community even before Paul's theological synthesis? In His predictions of the Passion, Jesus identifies Himself paradoxically as the "Son of Man" (Mk 8:31 par.). This title, which is found in the book of Daniel, designates a "corporate personality," a title which specifies the destiny of "the saints of the Most High." The new element in the message of Jesus is that the exaltation of the Son of Man is conditioned by his fulfilling the destiny of the Servant of Yahweh who is called to give his life as a sacrifice of expiation for the sake of the multitude (see Mk 10:45 and Is 53). If Jesus offers Himself as ransom for men it is not solely by substituting Himself for sinners *(anti pollōn,* [for many], Mk 10:45), but by performing the act which directs the destiny of His disciples.

The participation of the disciples in His suffering thus appears in the supernatural logic of the mission of Jesus, the Son of Man-Servant. Without going into a commentary on the narrative of the Last Supper,[29] let us simply remember the question asked by the mother of the sons of Zebedee. For her it was a matter of being assured that her sons would be associated with the glory of the Messiah as much as possible. "You do not know what you are asking. Are you able to drink the cup that I am to drink?" (Mt 20:22).[30] In a way, the cup and the baptism are unique; the disciples do not know what their response involves when they say: "We can."[31] The image of the cup is clarified by its biblical antecedents and points to "the divine wrath for sin which Jesus will undergo in place of the guilty."[32] Neverthless, the sons of Zebedee will participate in the fate of their Master: "The cup that I drink you will drink; and with the baptism with which I am to be baptized you will be baptized."

"This interpretation is in harmony with all of the preceding and subsequent gospel texts which accentuate insistently the responsibility of the disciples to carry their cross after their Master . . . The imitation of Christ is one of the foundations and one of the most remarkable characteristics not only of the teachings of the gospel but also of the ethics of the entire New Testament."[33]

This notion of participation accounts for the assurance which Jesus gives to His own. "A disciple is not above his teacher, nor a servant above his master; it is enough for the disciple to be like his teacher, and the servant like his master" (Mt 10:24-25). For those who persevere with Him in trials, Jesus states: "As my Father appointed a kingdom for me, so do I appoint for you that you may eat and drink at my table in my kingdom, and sit on thrones judging the twelve tribes of Israel" (Lk 22:29-30).

5. The Call to Follow Jesus: Intended for All

The Synoptic gospels indicate that Jesus chose a certain number of disciples, the Twelve and others, to form them into the beginnings of a New Israel and initiate them into his evangelical work. The verb *akolouthein* ("follow") has been faithfully preserved to designate this first stage of participation by the disciples in the life of their Master.

But as Th. Aerts notes,[34] it is arbitrary to limit this historical call to follow Jesus only to the missionaries and to account for every application to an individual case by a theology of the community *(Gemeindetheologie),* using the call of the rich young man as an example (Mk 10:17-22 par.).

Without going into details on this important point, let us at least indicate some principles for a solution. If, given His messianic consciousness, Jesus knew Himself to be the only one who could give the Life which His Father wanted to communicate to men, would He not have to invite all men to be converted to Him? "Come to me, all you who labor and are heavy laden, and I will give you rest. Take my yoke upon you, and learn from me, for I am gentle and lowly of heart, and you will find rest for your souls. For my yoke is easy and my burden is light" (Mt 11:28-30).

The exegesis of A. Schulz is false from its premise which rigidly equates "following Jesus" and "being called as a missionary." In reality, the gospels indicate a variety of uses for the verb *akolouthein* (follow), all of which indicate attachment to the person of Jesus, but they do not always denote a ministry.

The case of the woman of Galilee who followed the apostolic group is revealing (Lk 8:1-3; 23:49). They follow because of a personal choice on their part without being called to any particular ministry but simply because they believe in Jesus whom they consider to be "a prophet mighty in word and in work." The blind man of Jericho is another example. Jesus had said to him: "Go, your faith has saved you." Having recovered his sight, "he followed Him on the way," *(ēkolouthei autō en tē hodō,* Mk 10:52). We could not consider this a purely external following. The action expresses a personal attachment to Jesus.

It is true that the authors of the gospels did not combine the traditions with the intention of writing a biography, but with the catechetical purpose of enlightening the faithful in regard to their own Christian lives. One can often discern a parenetical intention. So Luke modifies the *logion* about carrying the cross by adding the word "daily" (Lk 9:23). The whole of Christian living is put under the sign of the cross. The process is striking in the long section describing the journey toward Jerusalem. Several times the evangelist stresses the participation of the multitude in this going up to Jerusalem (Lk 10:1: the 72 disciples; Lk 14:25: the multitudes).

Luke's intention is more evident when we recall that in the Acts he uses the title of "disciple" for Christians, even though such a title is not to be found in the Pauline *corpus*. He thus stresses the continuity between the case of the disciples who followed Jesus on the roads and the faithful who, because of the witness of the apostles, have accepted the "Way" of the Lord (see Acts 9:2).

It would be helpful to study how Mark expresses in his own way the continuity between the time of Jesus and that of the Church. Although he accepts the improbable thesis of the existence of a first edition to the second gospel which does not include the Passion narrative, E. Trocmé presents some interesting suggestions on this subject:

"In describing the manner in which Jesus had but recently trained His disciples to win over the Palestinian multitudes, the evangelist at the same time speaks of the present and also prophesies the future Christian mission which would be sustained and animated by the living Christ. The missionaries of his time and the multitudes to whom they spoke were "with Jesus," just as much as the Twelve (Mk 3:14) or the people (4:1) who had formerly been with Him."[35]

The conviction that the Christian life is a matter of being "with Jesus" is expressed most clearly by Matthew: only he portrays the son of Mary as Emmanuel, God with us (1:23). Gathered together in prayer, the disciples are assured of His presence (18:20). When he manifests Himself in glory as the Son of Man, He sends them out to the ends of the earth but assures them at the same time of His continual assistance: "And lo, I am with you always, to the close of the ages" (28:20). In Matthew's writings, on the redactional level, we should speak of a "with Jesus" mysticism.

Conclusion

The theme of following after Jesus is from its very beginnings far richer than could at first be guessed. It is not to be
identified only with the particular vocation of a few disciples
called to proclaim the Good News, but it implies a common
sharing of life with Jesus (Mk 3:4) and a participation in His
fate which gradually becomes clearer. To speak of "moral
imitation" weakens the sense of the texts; it is rather a matter
of His disciples' discovering in their daily contacts with the
Master a whole new set of life values.

As Son of Man, Jesus directs His call to all who are heavily
burdened by the formalism of traditional religion and trials of
this kind: "Come to me . . ." (Mt 11:28-29). Jesus first lived
the Beatitudes and His invitation is the desire He has to form
a family made up of persons who do the will of the Father and
are ready to give up everything in order to establish His Kingdom. Jesus not only spoke as a Master but also acted like a
good Shepherd who walks ahead of His flock to lead them to
the source of life. The development found in St. John will
simply specify the principle already laid down in the Synoptic
gospels.

C. Saint Paul

Unlike the Synoptic gospels in which "following after Jesus"
expresses fundamentally the characteristic proper of the disciple
(mathētēs), St. Paul never uses the verb "follow" *(akolouthein)*
in this sense any more than he presents himself as *mathētēs:*
he is the apostle of Christ crucified. On the other hand, he
does use the vocabulary of imitation: *"imitate," "imitator" (mi-
meomoi, mimētēs)*. We can discern the influence of the Greek
milieu in which the theme of imitation is prominent. It must
be noted that words of the root *mime-* have various nuances
since they express not only imitation but also reproduction
and representation.

Except for 1 Thes 2:14, which speaks of the imitation of
the churches in Judea, and Eph 5:1, which is concerned
with the imitation of God, the other texts refer to the imitation
of Christ by the apostle himself, while he in turn serves as a
model for the faithful.[36] "Be imitators of me as I am of Christ,"

is the principle which Paul so often reiterated. The epistle to the Hebrews presents for our imitation Christ who is pioneer and perfecter of our faith (12:2)—after having enumerated the examples furnished by the Old Testament (11), persevering Christians (6:12), and the heads of communities (13:7). There are other texts which, under different forms, also present Christ for our imitation (e.g., Phil 2:5).

1. The Imitation of Christ in the Theology of St. Paul

If we limit ourselves to a study of vocabulary, the theme of *imitatio Christi* holds a rather limited place in the thought of Paul. Paul seems to develop the theme mainly as a moral extension of a more fundamental principle, namely the union the believer must have with Christ. This is expressed in particular by the phrase *in Christo* (about 165 times) and by all the verbs composed with *sun* (with).

To understand the invitations to follow Christ, we must situate them within the context of man's vocation so well expressed in Rom 8:19: "For those whom He foreknew He also predestined to be conformed to the image of His Son, in order that He might be the first-born among many brethren." We also need to recall St. Paul's doctrine on baptism as a sacramental imitation of the death and resurrection of Christ.

This global doctrine of Paul's is presented in the articles of the DS, "Hommo dans le Christ"[37] and "Image et Ressemblance."[38] Without considering the entire content of Paul's teaching, we will focus on the following two points: *a)* On what aspects of Christ's life does Paul's imitation concentrate? *b)* How does Paul present himself as a "mediator" between the faithful and Christ?

a) What aspect of Christ's life does Paul imitate? Because of the circumstances of his vocation, Paul considers Christ primarily as the one who was once crucified but now lives in celestial glory as *Kyrios*. To the Corinthians who were tempted by the subtleties of human wisdom he says: "For I decided to know nothing among you except Jesus Christ and Him crucified" (1 Cor 2:2). This is why Paul refuses to make use of rhetorical devices; the naked word alone can witness to Him who emptied Himself on the cross in order to become for us "wisdom, righteousness and sanctification and redemption" (1 Cor 1:30).

Paul knows that he has been called to live this mystery of the death and resurrection of his Lord. He reveals himself in the second epistle to the Corinthians when he is required to defend his authority as apostle before his judaizing detractors:

"Always carrying in our body the death of Jesus, so that the life of Jesus may also be manifested in our bodies. For while we live we are always being given up to death for Jesus' sake, so that the life of Jesus may be manifested in our mortal flesh. So death is at work in us, but life in you" (2 Cor 4:10-12).

Already in 1 Cor 15:31, Paul writes: "I protest, brethren, by my pride in you which I have in Christ Jesus our Lord, I die every day *(kath' hēmeran),"* a statement which recalls the *logion* in Lk 9:23 about carrying the cross.

Paul points out the missionary significance of his sharing in the suffering of Christ: "Now I rejoice in my sufferings for your sake, and in my flesh I complete what is lacking in Christ's affliction for the sake of His body, that is, the Church" (Col 1:24).[39]

For all these texts, the word imitation is too weak: Paul does not imitate an external model but someone who lives in him. "I have been crucified with Christ; it is no longer I who live, but Christ lives in me; and the life I now live in the flesh I live by faith in the Son of God, who loved me and gave himself for me" (Gal 2:20).

Several authors (such as L. Cerfaux and A-M. Denis) have studied the way Paul applies the texts of the Servant of Yahweh in order to explain his mission. Cerfaux goes so far as to say that Paul considers himself as a "substitute" for Christ.[40] But the Apostle is too aware of Christ's dignity and His unique redemptive sacrifice to lay claim to such an independent role like that of standing in the place of the one judge. More accurately, David Stanley speaks of "a mystical concept of the apostolic vocation."[41]

   b) In some *parenetic contexts* we can infer an "ethical imitation." The clearest example of this is found in Phil 2:5-7:

"Have this mind among yourselves, which is in Christ Jesus, who, though He was in the form of God, did not count equality with God a thing to be grasped, but emptied Himself, taking the form of a servant, being born in the likeness of men. And being found in human form He humbled Himself and became obedient unto death, even death on a cross." More and more authors believe that in this passage Paul used a preexisting Christian hymn while adapting it for his own purposes.[42]

In order to bring the Philippians back to a unity of heart (having the same love, being in full accord and of one mind, 2:2), the Apostle invites them to reflect not on a particular example in the life of Christ, but rather on the most profound disposition of his existence: Christ's total submission to God from the Incarnation to Calvary. Paul obviously establishes here an antithesis between the action of the first and second Adam. The former wanted by his own power to attain the dignity of a god. Christ, on the contrary, renounces His privileges in order to share totally the human condition and accomplish perfectly the will of His Father. The disobedience of Adam is magnificently redeemed by the obedience of Christ (compare Rom 5:19).

Christ's obedience is evoked in the parenetic conclusion found in Rom 15:2-3: "Let each of us please his neighbor for his good, to edify him. For Christ did not please Himself, but as it is written, 'the reproaches of those who reproached thee fell on me.'" This quote from Ps 69, used in the Synoptic narratives of the Passion, indicates that Paul was familiar with this tradition, at least partially, and did not limit himself to proclaiming the mere fact of the cross. By declaring: "Christ did not please Himself," Paul touches the very roots of Christ's dispositions as Son. Untiringly he invites those who hear him to enter into this divine choice of renouncing self in order to live in the love of Him who redeemed us at the price of His own blood. In the same sense, Paul, appealing to this generosity, tells them of "the grace of our Lord Jesus Christ, who though He was rich, yet for your sake became poor, so that by His poverty you might become rich" (2 Cor 8:9), and justifies his appeal to mutual forgiveness by recalling that "as the Lord has forgiven you, so you also must forgive" (Col 3:13).

In Eph 4:32-5:2, it is God Himself who is proposed for the imitation of the faithful within a context that invites to mercy and pardon: "Be kind to one another, tenderhearted, forgiving

one another, as *(kathōs kai)* God in Christ forgave you. Therefore, be imitators of God, as beloved children. And walk in
love, as *(kathōs kai)* Christ loved us and gave Himself up for
us, a fragrant offering and sacrifice to God." As in Lk 6:35
one finds the same linking of the invitation to pardon after the
example of God with the quality of sonship. It is God's way of
acting that is proposed as the basis of man's way of acting. It is
possible to hesitate on the exact meaning of "as" *(kathōs kai)*.
Is it a simple comparison or an implication of causality? It
must be noted above all that the love of the Father is revealed
in the redemptive action of Christ who fulfilled for us the role
of Servant. "He was delivered up for us" alludes to Is 53. In
this same way are we to understand the development of Christ's
love for the Church which is patterned upon the love of a hus-
band for his wife (Eph 5:25-27): "Husbands, love your wives,
as Christ loved the Church and gave Himself up for her . . ."
Christ's manner of acting is not only a model but also a cap-
tivating power. By His sacrifice, He exorcized *eros* and revealed *agapē*.

To these texts must be added that of Heb 12:1-2: "Therefore, since we are surrounded by so great a cloud of witnesses,
let us also lay aside every weight and sin which clings so closely, and let us run with perseverance the race that is set before
us, looking to Jesus the pioneer and perfecter of our faith, who
for the joy that was set before Him endured the cross, despising
shame and is seated at the right hand of the throne of God."
The imitation referred to is not a matter of reproducing the
material gestures of Christ but of conforming to the spiritual
attitudes which He revealed. Son by baptism, the Christian must
become ever more truly what he already is.

From these statements we cannot conclude that Paul is not
interested in the human life of Christ. Still, a number of Protestant writers adopt this position by citing 2 Cor 5:16: "Even
though we once regarded Christ from a human point of view,
we regard Him thus no longer." Paul does not reject the Christ
of history as without value, but he opposes a knowledge "according to the flesh" (in the biblical sense of man left to his
own personal resources; see Mt 16:17; Gal 1:16) to a "spiritual" knowledge, that is a knowledge by faith which the Spirit
of God alone can communicate to us (see 1 Cor 12:1-2).

To say that Paul did not know "evangelical tradition" is an error which falsifies Paul's portrait. As several authors have shown, Paul often alludes to the teachings of Christ in his parenesis.[43] Follow Larsson, we confine ourselves to stating that Paul's teaching on baptism as death and resurrection with Christ could be related to Christ's call to follow Him by taking up his cross.[44] The Apostle would thus have adapted his statements to the situation of the community after Easter. "The paradoxical and expressive affirmations that one loses his life in 'following' Jesus so as to find it must have been particularly useful to explain what happens in the baptized at the time of their baptism" (p. 79). Research should be extended, using as a beginning the *logion* of the Passion compared to a baptism (Mk 10:38-39; see above); in a veiled manner Jesus let it be understood that after His death there would be a sacramental participation in His death.

Certain motivations of the parenesis presume a knowledge of the actual life of Christ. For example, 2 Cor 10:1: "I entreat you, by the meekness and gentleness of Christ." As A. Plummer remarks, "The appeal shows that St. Paul must have instructed the Corinthians as to the character of the Redeemer, whose words and actions must therefore have been known to himself."[45]

We can conclude that if Paul constantly refers to the kerygma of the Cross as the foundation of Christian life, it is not in the same manner in which R. Bultmann interprets Paul's message (the death of Jesus of whom Paul knows hardly anything except His crucifixion, but a death, nevertheless, which speaks of God condemning man's pride and challenging him to a life of naked faith). Rather, it is according to a mode profoundly rooted in history and transfigured by the resurrection and by liturgical celebration (see 1 Cor 11:23-24).

The Epistle to the Hebrews contains a parenetic development (5:7-8) on Christ's agony which can help us to grasp the purposes of which the gospel narratives of the Passion were composed and the death of Christ evoked in Eucharistic celebrations.

The concept of the *martyr* as one who imitates the passion of Christ is a very ancient one. It rests on the most obvious interpretation of Christ's word: "The cup that I drink, you will drink" (Mk 10:39). It is immediately illustrated in the story of Stephen in Acts 6-7 (compare especially Stephen's prayer with Jesus' last words on the cross, Lk 23:34 and 46) and finds its full flowering in Ignatius of Antioch and the Acts of the Martyrs.[46]

2. Paul as Model of the Faithful

In a way it is shocking to hear Paul affirm: "Be imitators of me, as I am of Christ." This explains why some commentators like W. Michaelis rob the text of its power by reducing it to a simple appeal to obedience. On the other hand, the specific force of the text has been brought to light by D. M. Stanley[47] and W. P. de Boer.[48]

This theme appears in the very first epistle of Paul to the Thessalonians, the oldest document on the Church. Referring to the circumstances surrounding the evangelization of the Thessalonians, Paul writes: "And you became imitators of us and of the Lord for you received the word in much affliction with joy inspired by the Spirit" (1 Thes 1:6). Subtly, Michaelis remarks that "and of the Lord" gives the impression of an addition made by Paul to his original thrust; the emphasis is thus placed on the imitation of the Apostle himself. The coexistence of affliction and joy is often found in the New Testament (e.g., Mt 5:11-12; Acts 4:31; 5:41 etc.), but it was particularly lived out by Paul. And so the conduct of the Thessalonians becomes an *example* for other communities (1 Thes 1:7-8: *typos*). This text shows that the gospel is not only a message but the power of God which unfolds through the action of the Spirit and demands the personal commitment of the one proclaiming.

By their attitude when confronted with persecution, the Thessalonian community "imitated the churches of God in Christ Jesus which are in Judea" (2:14). It is not simply a matter of comparison, as Michaelis understands it. Paul attaches great importance to the mother-community in Jerusalem, so he speaks of her to the Thessalonians. As Stanley sees it, "the experience of these Jewish Christians and their witness to Christ was included in Paul's version of the kerygma" (p. 868).

To admonish the idlers of Thessalonia who trouble the community by their exaggerated expectation of the parousia, Paul uses himself as an example. He worked with his hands to take care of his needs and to help the poor (2 Thes 3:6-9). He knows the gospel principle that the laborer is worthy of his salary (cited in 1 Cor 9:14). But to cut short all suspicion, he chooses to be a burden to no one and by his unselfishness he imitates Christ's own liberality (2 Cor 8:9). It is his personal manner of living the gospel (1 Cor 9:18).

The principle which justifies his appeal to imitation of him is expressed in 1 Cor 4:15-16. After distinguishing his role as apostle who lays the foundation for knowing Christ (3:11) and the role of those who build on this foundation, Paul affirms that he is not just any teacher but the very father of the community. "I became your father in Christ Jesus through the gospel in Christ Jesus. I urge you then, be imitators of me."

We must not sentimentalize the strength of this relatively rare affirmation: I became your father *(egennēsa)* in Christ Jesus. Paul knows well enough that only God can make of a man His own adopted son and yet he claims an active role in this new birth. He is not only an instrument through which the gospel reaches the ears of the converts, but he is the one who made use of all the resources of his mind and of his heart, who did not draw back from any sacrifice so that the seed might grow. To the Galatians, he compares this task of educating in the faith to the pains of childbirth: "until Christ be formed in you" (4:19).

These texts must not be given an affective interpretation as if the Apostle were animated by the very human desire that parents have to see their children resemble them. Paul's only ambition is to lead the faithful to Christ (2 Cor 5:5; 11:1-2). Paul knows only too well that when they turn aside from the model he has given them, the Corinthians turn to a counterfeit of the gospel (2:17; 4:2). Because of his function, he is so one with the message that he can speak of "his" gospel (Rom 16: 25; 1 Thes 1:5; 2 Thes 3:14).

David Stanley rightly concludes: "Thus, in Paul's view, if the divine truth of the gospel is unique and invariable (cf. Gal 1: 6-9), its transmission appears incarnated, so to speak, in the preacher's own Christian faith ... Paul's preaching does not only provide an occasion for the operation of the Spirit by faith in the hearts of his hearers. By its own characteristic modalities, which mirror Paul's own spirituality, it provides an objective norm against which the neo-Christian can measure his own experience of the Spirit of God."[49]

Paul does not present himself as an accomplished model, but gives the example of his efforts to attain Christ. "Brethren, I do not consider that I have made it my own (Christ as goal); but one thing I do, forgetting what lies behind and straining forward to what lies ahead, I press on toward the goal for the prize of the upward call of God in Christ Jesus ... join in imitating me and mark those who so live as you have an example of us" (Phil 3:13-14 and 17).

The text undoubtedly is one of the most revealing concerning Paul's mysticism. For Christ he has given up everything, even all the advantages of the Judiasm so dear to him (Phil 3:17); in order to gain Christ he has been willing to lose everything (the same antithesis is found in Mk 8:36, the *logion* about the demands made if one is to "follow" Jesus: "For what does it profit a man to gain the whole world and forfeit his life?"). What Paul desires passionately is "to know Christ and the power of His resurrection and share in His sufferings, becoming like Him in His death, that if possible I may attain the resurrection from the dead" (Phil 3:10-11).

All of the essential themes in St. Paul are brought together in this passage. We can then understand Paul's insistence that the Philippians follow his example and turn from those Judaizers who destroy the truth of the gospel.

Conclusion

a) There is such an intimate bond between spiritual fatherhood and the theme of imitation that Paul holds himself up as a "model" only to those churches which he himself has personally established (Thessalonica, Corinth, Philippi, Galatia. See Gal 4:12). In his epistle to the Ephesians, which seems to be a kind of circular letter, Paul urges, by contrast, the imitation of God and the imitation of Christ.

b) If Paul so insists on the obligation of the baptized to follow the model of their father in the faith, he shows the corresponding responsibility of preachers: they are not only to transmit the Word but they must first of all make its values manifest in their whole life.

c) The intimate bond which Paul establishes between personal imitation of him by the faithful and his own personal imitation of Christ is the strongest refutation of the opinion held by Michaelis which sees it merely as an appeal to obedience. Such a theme of imitation would find no support in Pauline texts. The imitation of Christ can never be understood in a purely human and volitional way, as when a person chooses the model he wants to imitate, but must be understood only within the context of grace and of *agapē* (Phil 3:13.17).

D. *The First Epistle of St. Peter*

The first epistle of St. Peter, too often overlooked by critics, is of interest because it gives a general survey of the essential catechetical themes and indicates the style of life of the first communities of Asia Minor just prior to the persecution of Nero. The Christology is centered on the figure of the Servant of Yahweh and it is with good reason that O. Cullmann has related it to the discourses of Peter in the Acts.[50] The allusions to the *verba Christi* are also numerous.[51] Let us look at this echo of the Beatitudes: "Now who is there to harm you if you are zealous for what is right? But even if you do suffer for righteousness' sake, you will be blessed" (1 Pt 3:13-14). "If you are reproached for the name of Christ you are blessed, because the spirit of glory and of God rests upon you" (4:14).

In a parenetic exhortation addressed to servants who are exposed to the mistreatment of their master, Peter writes: "For what credit is it, if when you do wrong and are beaten for it you take it patiently? But if when you do right and suffer for it you take it, you have God's approval. For to this you have been called *(eklēthēte)*, because Christ also suffered for you, leaving you an example *(hupogrammon)*, that you should follow in His steps" (2:20-21).

It has been suggested that the hymn which follows (2:22-23) is a liturgical text. It is inspired by Isaiah 53, which is certainly in harmony with the overall theology of this epistle. It is important to note the insistence Peter puts on Christ's way of acting during His Passion as the model for the slaves who, by the grace of Christ (v. 24b), are called upon to live His Passion anew in their daily existence. Why is it that R. Thysman rejects all references to the primitive theme of following Christ?[52]

The text contains the verbs "to call" and "to follow." Schulz on the other hand concludes that 1 Peter is the first text in the New Testament which presents the following of Jesus "as a *purely ethical* concept."[53] We do not consider this conclusion any better than the preceding. From the beginning the call to follow Jesus implied ethical demands and 1 Peter does not remain at a purely moral level but puts the imitation of the suffering Christ within the context of grace. The Passion is seen as the seal which verifies the authenticity of Christ's teaching. For this reason His Word is witness and power.

It is for the elders of the community to reincarnate the example of the Good Shepherd and to live with the same generosity and gift of self. This is the essential lesson of chapter 5:2-4: "Tend the flock that is your charge, not by constraint but willingly, not for shameful gain but eagerly, not as domineering over those in your charge but being an example to the flock *(tupoi tou poimniou)*. And when the chief Shepherd is manifested you will obtain the unfading crown of glory." It is easy to recognize Peter's remembrance of the words of Christ (Lk 22:25-27). The minister of the community should imitate Christ in order to lead the flock to the one Shepherd.

E. In St. John

A precise study of the theme of the imitation of Christ in the writings of St. John would demand a complete study of his gospel, his epistles and the Apocalypse. For our purpose, we will focus primarily on his gospel and limit ourselves to only a few references from the other Johannine writings.[54]

John states clearly his purpose in writing: "that you may believe that Jesus is the Christ, the Son of God, and that believing you may have life in His name" (Jn 20:31). This conclusion is to be related with the Beatitude which is found at the end of the first cycle of apparitions: "Blessed are those who have not seen and yet believe!" (20:29). The "joy of believing" is the particular characteristic of the Good News which Jesus communicated to His own. John's theology is dominated by the conviction that Jesus, because He is Son, is the manifestation of the Father (1:18) and that He has come into our world to draw believers into His Paschal journey from this world to the Father (See 13:1; 14:1-6).

Fashioned as a drama, the fourth gospel makes us enter into the conflict between darkness and Light and challenges us to opt for the Light while there is yet time (12:36). The faith which John wants to arouse and strengthen is not a simple confidence, nor the mere acceptance of a message, but rather a personal relationship which calls us out of ourselves. This is best expressed in the Johannine phrase "to believe in."[55]

From among the themes which express the nature of faith, we will use that of "walking in the company of Jesus" and we will see how this implies the desire for a community of life which grows through "imitation."

1. Following Jesus

Unlike Paul but in keeping with the Synoptics, John frequently uses the verb *akolouthein* (follow: 19 times) as well as the noun *mathētēs* (disciple). To understand the implications, we must remember that John's particular point of view is to relate the time of the Church to the time of Jesus or, if one prefers, to point out the enduring actuality of the earthly life of Jesus. Because of that, the word "disciple" can mean the men Jesus called to himself along the banks of the Jordan or in Galilee, as well as all those who would believe in him because of their witness. This Johannine use of the word corresponds to the use found in Acts.[56]

Only in rare cases is *akolouthein* used with a purely physical meaning. Even in 6:2—"And a multitude followed him *(ēkolouthei)* because they saw the signs which he did on those who were diseased"—the context gives evidence that in spite of very imperfect dispositions, the crowds fell under the spell of the attraction of Jesus' personality and expected from him some superior manifestation.[57] It is not only a taste for the miraculous but a search for the will of God: "What must we do, to be doing the works of God?" (6:28).

This religious meaning of "following" is well illustrated by an old rabbinic commentary on this passage from Exodus: "The people believed in the Lord and in His servant Moses" (14: 31): "Because of this faith by which they believed in me, it was fitting that I divide the sea for them. Since they did not say to Moses: How can we possibly go into the desert since

we have absolutely no provision for the journey, but rather
they believed and followed Moses."[58]

The most characteristic uses of the verb *follow* are found in
the vocation narratives. Because of the witness given by the
Baptist, two disciples followed Jesus (1:37). When Jesus
asked: "Whom do you seek?", they replied: "Rabbi, where do
you live?" This brief dialogue contains in germ form the great
themes of the gospel: seek, follow, dwell. "Following" Jesus
thus appears to be the fundamental attitude of the disciple between his initial discovery in faith and the consummation of
union in the kingdom (8:35; 14:3; etc.). As in the Synoptic
gospels, the decisive word of calling is "Follow me" *(akolouthei
moi,* 1:43). The context shows that this "following" is not
primarily one's commitment to a mission but a movement toward the progressive discovery of the mystery of Jesus. From
this comes the importance of confessions of faith some of
which are charged with post-paschal fulness (thus, in chapter 1: "Lamb of God," "him of whom spoke Moses and
the prophets," "the Son of God," "the King of Israel," "the
Son of Man"). Intimacy with Jesus, which unveils for His
"friends" the most profound secrets, lies at the heart of following Jesus;[59] from this point of view, "the disciple whom
Jesus loved" bears singular testimony. If it imposes great demands, "following" Jesus should not be confused with obedience. While the latter can sometimes be only an external submission without the heart's allegiance, "following" can only be
realized in the climate of preferential love expressed by the
verb *agapan.*

In the fourth gospel, the call to follow Jesus emerges as
necessary to salvation. "I am the light of the world; he who
follows me will not walk in darkness, but will have the light
of life" (8:12; see also 12:35-36).

The theme of Light which is fundamental to the Johannine
corpus, encompasses simultaneously God's revelation to the
world of salvation given in Christ and the quality of the life
of the believer. "Jesus, the Light of the world, dispels not
only the darkness of ignorance but also that of sin and death,
giving life to those who conform their actions to his revelation."[60]

The allegory of the Good Shepherd brings important precision to this doctrine. "The shepherd calls his own sheep by name and leads them out. When he has brought out all his own, he goes before them, and the sheep follow him, and they know his voice. A stranger they will not follow" (10:3-5). In the doctrinal richness of this passage one finds again the great Johannine themes: the Father's initiative (=the doorkeeper), the "inner sensitivity" necessary to perceive Christ's call, the personal (v. 14: "I know my own and my own know me."), and communal structure of faith (v. 16: "there shall be one flock"), the decisive role of Christ who alone can give life in abundance (v. 10). A new harmonic appears: sacrifice. "The good shepherd lays down his life for his sheep" (v. 11). The link between the sheep who follow and the goodness of the Shepherd is not yet explicit; the texts that follow will show that the behavior of the sheep is determined by the discovery of Christ's *agapē*.

This common goal which ought to exist between Christ and His own is manifested most clearly on Palm Sunday. "The hour has come for the Son of man to be glorified. Truly, truly, I say to you, unless a grain of wheat falls into the earth and dies, it remains alone; but if it dies, it bears much fruit" (12:23-24). A comparison of this parable with that of the sower found in the Synoptic gospels is most instructive; the seed that comes forth is not a Word detached from the one who speaks it, but is the very Messenger of God. Word and Life are indissolubly linked in the person of Jesus.

As is the case in the Synoptic gospels, the revelation of the absolute necessity of the Passion is followed immediately by a call to all: "He who loves his life loses it, and he who hates his life in this world will keep it for eternal life" (Jn 12:25).[61] As we have shown, following N. A. Dahl, for the Synoptics, the theme of *imitatio Christi* is directly related to that of *sequela Christi*. To follow Christ is to give everything.

In verse 26, this doctrine is applied to the servants of Christ in the work of salvation: "If anyone serves me *(diakonē)*, he must follow me *(akoloutheito)*; and where I am, there shall my servant *(diakonos)* be also." With N. Lazure, we believe that *diakonos* must be given the profound theological meaning that it has acquired in the New Testament. Further light is shed on our text by the declaration of 13:16: the one sent by Christ must share the lot of his master. There is no mission without sharing in sacrifice.

The call to "follow" Jesus tends to be specified as an invitation to "martyrdom." What Peter was unable to do before the Passion (13:36), he will do later on: "Another will gird you and carry you where you do not wish to go . . . Follow me" (21:18-19). A pastoral function can be fulfilled only within the context of love for Christ—"Simon, do you love me?" (Jn 21:15-17)—and must lead to a total gift of self like unto that of the Good Shepherd.

This theme is not found in this form in John's epistles and *akolouthein* ("follow") is found only once in Revelation (14: 4). It concerns the virgins "who follow the Lamb wherever He goes." Such a vision does not refer exclusively to one group of ascetics in opposition to the rest of the Christian community, but presents the Church in its totality as the body of the redeemed who have refused all compromise with the Beast and live in undivided fidelity. One should also consider the texts which apply to Christians the mission of "witness" by imitating Christ "the faithful Witness (Ap 1:5, 3:14).

The theme of "following Christ" in John's gospel is one that is extremely rich. In his doctrinal dissertation which we have used extensively,[62] A. Weers could have given more stress to the relationship between "following" and "imitation." If likenesses between John's perspective and the Synoptic tradition are not wanting, it is fitting to note also the differences. John does not stress the unique demands made in order to follow Christ, like detachment from riches, family, etc, but he is satisfied with general statements: to walk in the light, to walk in the truth. In particular, he emphasizes the importance of "faith" in order to follow Him who presents Himself as the Way (Jn 14:6). "To follow" Jesus and "to believe in Him" become almost identical as can be seen if one compares 8:12 with 12:35-36. Nevertheless, the theme of "walking after Jesus," because of its imagery brings out the dynamism of the Christian life and the impact of faith on the totality of a person's way of life.

With N. Lazure, we can conclude: "The verb *to follow* goes beyond a particular attitude towards life, like faith or love. Rather, it possesses a wider significance because it outlines for the disciple a way of life and synthesizes for him the ideal of discipleship: a complete sharing in the life, destiny and mission of the Lord, as well as an entry into intimacy with Him."[63]

2. The Example of Jesus

a) The washing of the feet

Only John relates an episode in which Jesus explicitly makes Himself an example: "If I then, your Lord and Teacher, have washed your feet, you also ought to wash one another's feet. For I have given you an example *(hupodeigma)*, that you should also do as I have done to you" (13:14-15).

A literary analysis of this passage brings to the fore a two-fold center of concern: one prophetic and the other moral. Regarding the first, Jesus by doing the work of a slave "mimes" in a way His own Passion and gives us to understand that He accepts His sufferings as "Servant of Yahweh." From this point of view Christ's gesture is beyond imitation; only the Lamb of God can take away the sin of the world. And if someone wishes to "have part" with Him in the eschatological kingdom he must by faith consent to a purification of which the waters used in the washing of the feet are a symbol.

As several commentators have pointed out, John, by narrating the washing of the feet instead of the institution of the Eucharist, intended to highlight "the inner meaning" of the Eucharist, having already put the words of institution in the discourse on the Bread of Life (6:51b). Christ's sacrifice transforms the meaning of existence by revealing new values, those of service (comp. Jn 13:13-15 with Lk 22:25-27) and brotherhood. "The sacrament is effective only if the mind of Christ takes possession of the disciple. The commandment 'Do this in memory of me' is thus conditioned by the words of Christ: 'You call me Lord and Master and you do so rightly, for so I am. If then I have washed your feet . . . you also must do the same.' "[64]

The "service" to which Christ by His example thus commissions His own, takes on various forms: material service and spiritual ministry (13:16). "A servant is not greater than his master, nor is he who is sent *(apostolos)* greater than he who sent him." This is the only passage in John's gospel where the word *apostolos* is found and it must be inter-

preted in the light of the verses which follow (17:18 and
20:21). The context (the priestly prayer and the intimate
setting of the Upper Room) bring out the closeness of Christ's
relationship with those whom He sends to fulfill His Father's
design for unity. "Having become one with the Father and
the Son by their faith in Christ and receiving from the Risen
One His Holy Spirit, the apostles can now truly be 'missioned,'
with Christ's very own mission."[65]

b) To love as Jesus loves

The special dimension of "service" into which Jesus initiates
His own by His passage from this world to the Father (13:1)
is made clear in the discourse after the Last Supper. The
thought which is constantly repeated is the notion that the Son
acts as the Father, and that the disciples in turn are to act as
the Son.

Here is the most telling passage: "A new commandment I
give to you, that you love one another; even as (kathō) I have
loved you, so you must love one another. By this all will know
that you are my disciples if you have love for one another"
(13:34-35).

In qualifying this commandment as "new," Jesus does not
forget that the Old Testament commanded love of neighbor,
but in this moment of farewell, He makes of this one commandment of love the distinctive sign of the covenant for which he
consecrates Himself to God.[66]

The element which specifies agapē is the phrase "as I have
loved you." The conjunction kathōs can be interpreted in a
comparative sense and in a causal sense. The evangelist deliberately uses words with their double meaning. The love of
Christ for His own appears simultaneously as the model of
unselfish love and as its cause: unless one dwells in Christ, he
cannot love as Christ loves (see 15:4-5, 9-10). The love which
the disciples are called to live among themselves should be a
"transparency" of the love of Christ and, like Christ's love, lead
to the Father. Such a conclusion is strengthened if one considers the texts of John which speak of the "fruit" to be produced. Because Christ consents to die like the grain of wheat,
He bears much fruit (12:24), and this fruit is the love of his

disciples who are grafted onto Him like the branches onto the vine.

3. The Imitation of God in Jesus Christ

In a general way, John shows Christ to us as the one who reveals the Father both by His word and by His action. And so to justify a cure on the Sabbath day, Jesus says: "My Father works and I also work" (5:17). A short parable, which C. H. Dodd aptly presents of an apprentice who lets his father guide him in order to "make his way into the business," captures the meaning of this text: "The Son can do nothing of His own will but only what He sees the Father doing; for whatever He does, that the Son does likewise. For the Father loves the Son and shows Him all that He is doing" (Jn 5:19-20).[67]

The perfect communion of thought (e.g. 8:16; 12:49-50), of will (8:28-29), of love (14:30) between the Son and the Father becomes for the disciple the *imitatio Dei,* the imitation of God that is revealed in Jesus Christ. This doctrine explains why in many passages of John's epistles we cannot tell whether the author is proposing for our imitation the Father or Christ.[68]

The unity of the Father and the Son in the richness of their Trinitarian life appears finally as the ultimate norm of unity that Christians must envision: "That they may be one; even as you, Father, are in me, and I in you, that they also may be in us, so that the world may believe that you have sent me" (17:21). It would be enlightening at this point to reflect on the role of the Spirit in the realization of this unity. Let us note that John has stressed more the action of the divine *Pneuma* as "the Spirit of truth" who leads to a more perfect knowledge of Christ, and as "the Spirit of life" who assures the rebirth of believers than the role of the Spirit of love as that which enables us to love as Christ loves.

Conclusion

Already the theme of "following" Jesus manifested the community of destiny linking Christ and His own. By putting the washing of the feet at the beginning of his Passion narrative, John introduces us into the most profound meaning of this drama—serving the multitude—and leads us to discover the consequences in our own life. The imitation of Christ ("I have given you an example") as it is presented in John's gospel does not consist in literally repeating gestures but takes place at the level of those dominant trends which direct life. On this point, we find profound accord with St. Paul.

In his dissertation, A. Weers quite rightly recognizes that, despite its inadequacies, the concept of imitation was necessary in order to express one aspect of the relationship between the disciples and the Master. In reaction to "a certain concern to preserve at the heart of apostolic activities what is called the interior life,"[69] he insists in a one-sided way on the importance of imitation in fulfilling one's mission. Without a doubt, the Christian must imitate Christ in fraternal service and zeal to form a true community. The minister of the gospel must "follow" the Master in the gift of self, yet in John's gospel the mission is never separated from the union (expressed by the verb *menein,* "to abide in").

Even if the philological analyses of J. Radermakers, which carefully distinguish between *pempō* (stressing the interior aspect of mission) and *apostellō* (stressing the one being sent into the world), seem quite subtle, his conclusion puts in focus an essential facet of John's message: "The mission of the Son sent by the Father is the soul and profound purpose of the apostolate. It makes every Christian life apostolic to the extent that the believer attends to (listens and sees) God's revelation, that is, to the extent that he contemplates the work of the Father. The 'apostolate' is simply the activation, the translation, the communication through human action, of this fundamental intention of the very love of God. The apostle does the work of the Father."[70] To be authentic, the *imitatio Christi* in the service of others must be lived in the spirit of Christ: in constant relationship to the Father.

Chapter II

The Spiritual Tradition

by Canon Etienne Ledeur

It is simply impossible to present within the limitations of an article a complete view of the spiritual tradition on a subject so vast and popular as the imitation of Christ. It would be necessary to draw not only on the lives of the saints and spiritual writings but also on the liturgy and preaching that considers this theme, the catechisms and other forms of Christian instruction, the witnesses of the actual living out of this imitation of Christ in daily life as well as in situations of crisis. But we must limit ourselves to a few soundings.

Another major difficulty is the fact that the concept of imitation in its various forms lacks precision; it can range from mimicry to union, even though the authors do not say this in so many words. Imitation is immediately linked to the teaching and example of Christ in His Gospel, with Christ the Model and Mediator. We have already seen how it is presented in Scripture as a following of Christ. Even though many understand it as a way of acting in the moral sphere ("imitate the virtues of Christ"), it is clear to the more serious that it is not so limited: we imitate Christ when we live in His Spirit, when we identify with the interior dispositions He has towards His Father or towards persons. Finally, the principal modes of Christian life (marriage, religious life, virginity, monasticism, apostolate, priesthood), like every spiritual state,[1] are directly related to the imitation of Christ. For this reason we will focus on only a few succinct themes of different types chosen from the unfolding history of the Church, so as to expose the rich diversity hidden in the imitation of Christ.

A. Early Christianity: The Martyr

It is the desire to "follow Christ," to become His true disciple, to achieve with Him a likeness to God, which explains in the first centuries of the Church the reality and the doctrine of martyrdom, of virginity, of the spiritual combat in the desert, and finally of monasticism. Since we are unable to address ourselves to each of these forms of imitation of Christ,[2] we choose to present only that of the martyr. It is well known that the other forms of imitation of Christ mentioned above have often been presented as substitute forms for physical martyrdom. The two scriptural phrases "to follow" and "to imitate" Jesus will soon be used with predeliction to designate and understand martyrdom. It is natural that these appear from the pen of those relating the facts and the theologians who attempt to penetrate their meaning.[3]

1. Saint Stephen[4]

Actually, these phrases (to follow, to imitate) are not found in the story of Stephen related in Acts (chaps. 6-7). But a relationship is found by comparing the death of Christ with that of the first Christian martyr, not primarily in the account of the actual concrete circumstances (arrest, the hasty trial, recourse to false witnesses, etc.) but by looking at Stephen's witness and prayer before his death. He professes to see "the heavens open and the Son of Man standing at the right hand of God" (Acts 7:56).[5] Also, the final prayer of Jesus on the cross directly inspires the apostle as he is being stoned: "Lord Jesus, receive my spirit . . . do not hold this sin against them" (Acts 7:59-60; Lk 23:34, 46).

The above is sufficient to be able to say that the first generation of Christians is conscious that "the judgment of Jesus . . . explains the history of the Church because it continues in the person of the disciples of Jesus whom the world condemns."[6] We see in the death of the first martyr a replica of the death of Jesus, and in his witness and his pardon the same sentiments as those of Jesus on the cross.

Without going into a discussion here about the account in Acts, let it suffice to say that exegetes generally agree that the narrative rests on a very old source which was integrated into the Acts during the post-apostolic age.

Tradition has a particular esteem for the martyrdom of Stephen.[7] St. Cyprian says: "Such needed to be the first martyr of Christ . . . he was not only a preacher of the Passion of the Lord but, even more, an imitator of His most patient gentleness."[8] The liturgical books retain the same message: Stephen was "an imitator of the Lord's charity," "a true follower of Christ" as he interceded for his persecutors.[9]

2. St. Ignatius of Antioch († c. 110-117)[10]

St. Ignatius of Antioch is the first Christian who transmits to us in his writings the thoughts and sentiments that were his at the very time he awaited martyrdom. His letter to the Romans is probably the most outstanding because of the expressed intensity of his desire to be with Jesus Christ and, for that reason, to be like Him: "May I not only speak but may I also will . . . in this way I shall not only be called a Christian but also prove to be one"; "At last I am well on the way to being a disciple"; "Permit me to be an imitator of my suffering God."[11]

It seems improbable that one could "present the reflections made by the bishop of Antioch about his martyrdom without even mentioning Christ" and think that for him "the passion of a martyr has value in itself as did that of Christ."[12] There is no martyrdom without Christ: "Near the sword, near to God; with the beasts, with God; only let it be in the name of Jesus Christ. To suffer with Him I endure all things if He who became perfect man gives me the strength."[13] For Ignatius, Jesus is the essential reference point, motivation, source, and goal. It is, therefore, incorrect to insist upon dualist or gnostic influences in explaining Ignatius' thoughts on life and on death.

But Ignatius is familiar with an imitation of Christ other than that of martyrdom. If he says that Christians imitate God when they are generous and charitable (Eph 1; Trall 1), it is the historical Christ he has in mind when he exhorts the Churches to be patient in times of trial and to be united around their bishop: "Let us strive to imitate the Lord" (Eph 10);

"Cherish unity, shun divisions, do as Jesus Christ did for He, too, did as the Father did."[14] The thought is clear: Jesus is the model; the Christian must be inspired by His example. Although Ignatius sees martyrdom as the final imitation of the death of Christ, he does not ignore the fact that the Christian life itself is already a participation in the passion of Christ. And so he congratulates the Smyrnites for being by their unshakeable faith, as it were, "nailed body and soul to the cross of the Lord Jesus Christ, and well established in love through the blood of Christ" (*Smyrn.* 1). He likewise says of himself: "My carnal love has been crucified."[15] Christ is in fact "our life inseparable" (Eph 3): "Let us then do everything remembering that He lives in us" (Eph 15). Union awakens the desire to be conformed to the one loved. This is evident in Ignatius' recommendations for the conduct of the Churches, as in his understanding of the martyrdom which awaits him through which union and conformity will be achieved.

3. The Acts of the Martyrs

The Acts of the Martyrs, a literary genre which is both varied and extensive, can furnish us with a witness that is useful to our purpose: How did the writers understand and present the emotions and thoughts of these martyrs? How did they present these to their readers? Our probing can begin with a few authentic documents written prior to the year 200. If the Acts of St. Justin and his companions and that of the Scillitan Martyrs of this period make no allusion to the imitation of Christ, it must be noted that these are only a kind of report on their trials. On the other hand, the narrative of St. Polycarp's martyrdom puts in bold relief the resemblance between Christ's passion and that of the martyr and specifies twice, once at the beginning and once at the end, that all of these events "happened so that our Lord could exhibit to us anew the type of martyrdom narrated in the gospel," so that we might all "imitate the martyrdom which was in accord with the gospel of Christ."[16] A few years later we have the letters from the churches of Lyons and Vienna to the churches of Asia and Phrygia which speak in much the same way: "All of the confessors strove to imitate Christ who though being divine did not boast of it. They gladly conceded the name of martyrdom to Christ. They neither proclaimed themselves as martyrs nor did they permit others to address them as martyrs . . ."[17] A new insight appears in these letters: not only do the martyrs "imitate" Christ, but it is actually Christ who suffers in them. "Sanctus was washed and fortified by the heavenly streams of living waters which spring forth from the side of Christ . . . Christ suffered in him."[18]

4. Exhortation to the Martyrs: Origen and Cyprian

A few documents written during the centuries of persecution show how the Church prepared Christians for eventual martyrdom. The two best known ones were composed by Origen of Alexandria a little before the year 250,[19] and by St. Cyprian on the outskirts of Carthage in 253 or 257.[20] These two works differ both in length and in exegetical methodology. Origen employs comparative and allegorical exegesis while Cyprian simply quotes, often at great length, from the texts of the two Testaments.

Neither of these exhortations is founded on the idea that the martyr imitates Jesus Christ; despite the extensive use of biblical texts many are not used that one would expect to find, such as the hymn in the Epistle to the Philippians. Nevertheless, the thought of Christ is constantly present. Cyprian knows that the Lord "has challenged us not only by His words but by His actions, having suffered . . . and having been crucified so as to teach us to suffer and die according to His example."[21] The theology of martyrdom in Origen is more elaborate and much richer. He recalls, for instance, that "we have received the covenants of God by agreement," one of which is "living according to the gospel." This rests on the conditions imposed if one follows Jesus (Mt 16:24-25). Because of our baptism "we must deny ourselves . . . and say: I live, now not I" (Gal 2:20). Let us see whether or not we bear our cross; let us know what to expect if Christ lives in us.[22] The idea that martyrdom signifies "our own cross" and that it is this cross which enables us to follow Christ is found several times. It is Christ who guides us,[23] who leads us,[24] who walks with us.[25] In other places, martyrdom is related to Christ's temptation in the desert, to the baptism of blood which He longed for,[26] to the chalice which He drank.[27]

"For us, Jesus gave up His life, and we must give up ours."[28]

Beginning with this likeness in sacrifice, Origen develops a likeness in the glory which awaits the martyr of Christ.[29] It is in this context that the word *imitator* appears.[30] Origen's enthusiasm for martyrdom is well known. We see that he relies on a noble conception of conformity to which the martyr is called; the martyr enters into communion with the mystery of Christ, and it is from this vantage point that Origen speaks of imitation. We could say that for him martyrdom is a soteriological mystery realized in mystical union with Christ through the baptism of sacrificial death.

Cyprian's theology is not so rich. Together with his *Exhortation to Martyrdom,* his letter to the people of Thibar delineates more clearly the thought that the martyr is an imitator of Christ.[31]

We could multiply notes and references. If a doctrine can be drawn from the writings of the first Christian centuries on the subject of martyrdom, it is this: "The martyrs draw near to our Lord who died for all people as much because of their great love as because they were made like unto Him by their sufferings."[32] Martyrdom is the fruit of "following" Christ and of charity; this is what gives it its meaning. We could say that in these ancient texts, the emphasis is not put on imitation of Christ in the sense that Christ went to His passion and the Christian must become a martyr *in order to* be like Him. The Christian must be faithful to his vocation and to his faith; this fidelity could lead to martyrdom. The Christian then finds himself "placed with Christ" and at the same time finds himself in His likeness and so strives to imitate Him. Speaking of the martyr Stephen, Ireneaus writes: "He fulfilled the perfect precept, imitating in every way the Master who gave us the example of martyrdom . . ."[33] In these texts the delicate nuance of communion with another, of participation in the mystery of Christ, puts definitely into a secondary place an imitation that is moral, voluntary, and above all material.[34]

B. Two Doctors of the Church: John Chrysostom and Augustine

1. St. John Chrysostom (†407)

St. John Chrysostom, "above all a moralist, . . . sought primarily to form his listeners to Christian life and virtue."[35] In order to define this life and these virtues and move Christians to virtuous living, he finds his best argument in the life and virtues of Christ. One could object that the *Letters to Olympias* or *The Comparison of a King and a Monk* hardly mention Jesus. But these are exceptions. Habitually, reference to Jesus Christ comes spontaneously to John's thought. This corresponds for him with the intention the Father had in giving His Son as an example to the world of an unselfish athlete, one superior to us. Such also is Christ's intention.

"The actions which Christ did that were like ours He did not accomplish only to confirm His incarnation but also to form us in virtue. If in all things He had acted as God, how could we have known how to act when we found ourselves in difficult circumstances?"[36] John Chrysostom explains this pedagogy of Christ: "I have given you this example that as I have acted with you, you too must act with each other. Do you not see that many of Christ's actions were done to be an example to us? A master paces himself to the falterings of little children as they learn to read. His hesitation is not due to ignorance on his part but is an evidence of the solicitude he has for the children. So too with Christ; His actions were not the consequence of imperfection in His nature but a condescension."[37]

Christ acting in this way is reassuring: "Just as a person who must walk an untravelled road enters upon it more easily and with greater enthusiasm if he perceives that someone has gone before him, so it is with walking in the way of the commandments; those who know someone goes on before them follow more easily. In order that our human nature might follow with greater readiness, Christ took on our flesh and our nature; He walked the way before us and has shown us the commandments translated into action."[38]

A sermon on the Passion develops this idea at length: "By His coming, Christ intended to form persons in the practice of all virtues. So whoever desires a like destiny cannot be content with words only but must translate these into action because knowledge gained through experience is the most efficacious . . . This is why our Saviour, having come to form us in the practice of all virtues, while telling us what we must do, begins Himself by doing it. 'He who joins together teaching and example,' He said 'will be called great in the kingdom of heaven.'

See then: He makes meekness and humility a precept and formulates it; consider how he instructs us by his example. In these words: 'Blessed are the poor in spirit; blessed are the meek,' He shows us how we are to practice humility. How does he show us? Having taken a towel, He washed the feet of His disciples. What humility can compare with this? It is no longer by His words but by His acts that He teaches us."[39]

There follow seven exhortations formulated in the same pattern: the command of Christ, the example of Christ. Thus can a Christian know his obligation: gentleness and patience, prayer for his enemies, doing good to them, poverty, the way to pray, humility, consent to the Father's will.

Referring to Christ is a very conscious process for John Chrysostom. We find a number of finely constructed phrases which he uses to express the necessity of imitating Christ. "You are a Christian in order to imitate Christ and obey His commands. Look then to Him who is the perfect model."[40] "In order to exhort His disciples to great things, Our Lord Jesus Christ gave Himself as an example."[41] "May Christ never cease making Himself known in us. How will He make Himself known? By the actions we perform in imitation of Him."[42] "Be then, I encourage you anew, imitators of Christ. Such an imitation is possible for us; it lifts us above our human nature and renders us like unto God."[43] "Christ has given you the means to become like Him. Do not then fear to imitate Him. Fear rather the possibility of not becoming like Him."[44]

Whether he looks at Christ directly in the gospel or through the Acts or St. Paul, John Chrysostom points out what Christ has done and draws a lesson from it. "If Christ has come from heaven to instruct us it is so that our thought might be lifted up to heaven and we might be imitators of Him to the extent that this is possible. And how, we might ask, is it possible for us to become imitators of Christ? . . . in doing all we can for the common good and in not seeking our own interests. Jesus Christ, says St. Paul, did not seek Himself."[45]

The parallel between what one sees in the life of Christ and what is seen in the life of the Christian is at times distressing: "Your Master was crucified and do you seek rest? Your Master was pierced with nails and do you lead a life of comfort? Did not your Master die on a cross? You cannot die in this same

way. At least imitate His example in some other way. Crucify
your own selves if no one crucifies you. Crucify yourself not by
taking your life, for this would be a crime, but in the sense
intended by St. Paul when he said: 'The world is crucified to
me and I to the world'."[46]

In another place John Chrysostom's thought is delicately
nuanced: "So that we might not in all circumstances either be
afraid of giving scandal or become indifferent, Christ has given
us limits and rules so that we might act in one way or another
as occasion demands." He does not uphold the Judaic observ-
ances regarding food, but He does insist that Peter pay the
tax of a drachma.[47]

All categories of Christians must be conformed to Jesus
Christ. Thus, as applied to pastors, the gospel story of the
Samaritan woman indicates the "school" in which apostoles are
to be formed.[48] Christ's progressive method of teaching is
given as an example: "Christ imposed these rules and laws
on his disciples so that they might act with great compassion
once they in turn would have the peoples of the whole earth
as their disciples."[49]

Are these texts primarily ascetical without a touch of the
mystical? This objection has been made about the writings of
John Chrysostom before his ordination.[50] We must not be left
with this as a final impression. The early monk who remained
an ascetic while at the same time becoming priest and bishop
was animated with a profound love of Christ. It is from this
love that the works of a Christian must spring: "No one can
impose another foundation other than that which has been
laid down from the beginning. Let us then build on Christ so
that He alone is our foundation as the vine is for the branches;
and may nothing come between Christ and us. At the slightest
separation, we die instantly. And let us not be only attached
to Christ, let us be united to Him and let us unite ourselves to
Him by action."[51]

More than any other Father of the Church, John Chrysostom
was captivated by St. Paul's notion of incorporation into
Christ.[52] The expression "to put on Christ" has for him a very
real connotation. Born of the earth and earthly in Adam, we
receive in baptism the image of the heavenly Man, Christ.[53]
The *forma Christi* is given to each Christian and is the bond of

unity among all: "You have put on Christ . . . you are all one in Christ Jesus . . . You have only one model, one pattern, Christ . . . Those who formerly were but Greeks, or Jews, or slaves, now come forward, taking on the form, not of an angel or archangel, but that of the Master of all things; behold, in themselves they show forth Christ."[54]

The relationship between incorporation and imitation is also expressed in regard to Christian life: "Behold our Head. Let us ponder what head it is of which we form one body, the head to which we submit ourselves. Because of such a leader, we must be even better than angels and archangels since we have honors bestowed on us greater than theirs . . . Christ has become our head . . . and we must bear this in mind . . . if you are the body of Christ, bear the cross, as He did."[55]

Exhortations to benevolence and almsgiving are often based on this conviction, and this in a two-fold way: Christ being our head, we must imitate the love He has for us; Christ being the head of our brothers, since there is but one head and one body, we must come to the help of Christ's members.

"We have a name that is greater than all others and which is common to us all—the name of Christian—of body, of child and of friend of God . . . We who are called by the name of the King of the universe . . . and are members, He being our head, ought we not to make every effort to walk in His footsteps?"[56]

"The Father gave up even His only Son: and you do not even give a piece of bread to Him who delivered and immolated Himself up for you . . . He was delivered up for you, immolated for you, He lives in want for you, He gives you of his good things for your use and you do not give in the same manner?"[57]

Surely we could have shown more precisely the connection between incorporation and imitation by looking at baptismal catecheses and instructions on the Eucharist. John Chrysostom insists more on the disposition of those who share the Eucharist and upon its fruit in their lives than on the mystery itself. At baptism, the Christian receives the yoke of Christ: "Take upon you my yoke and learn. Learn, that is to say: give ear so that you can learn of me. What I expect of you is not burdensome: you who are my servants, imitate me who am your Master; you who are but dust and ashes learn from the example of Him who created heaven and earth and who even formed you. Learn

of me that I am meek and humble of heart. Yes, the one who
has taken upon himself the yoke of Christ and has learned to
be meek and humble of heart will be seen to possess all virtues
and will walk in the footsteps of the Master."[58] John Chrysostom teaches Christians "the imitation of Jesus Christ as the
integrating center for the ideal of Christian perfection."[59]

2. St. Augustine (†430)

A precise synthesis of the imitation of Christ according to
St Augustine has been presented elsewhere.[60] Here we will
simply point out references to a few typical passages from different contexts in which Augustine develops his doctrine of the
imitation of Christ.[61]

C. The Middle Ages

"Beginning with the 12th century and the development of
the doctrine of Christ's humanity, which . . . will become one of
the characteristics of medieval devotion, asceticism both in its
positive and negative aspects becomes primarily an asceticism
of conformity to the mysteries of Christ's earthly life."[62] We
must be content here to see how this view is nuanced when it
becomes explicit in two of the greatest saintly persons of the
Middle Ages, Bernard of Clairvaux and Francis of Assisi.

1. St. Bernard (†1153)

Saint Bernard, as all authors like to recognize, gives to
Christ the role of Mediator. For him, the restoration of resem-
balance to the Word in man is brought about through the media-
tion of Jesus.[63] Christ incarnate is "the way of humility which
leads to truth," whether Bernard envisions it as man's return to
God or whether he begins with the Trinity and the movement
is a descent toward man.[64] In *On the Love of God*,[65] he presents meditation on the mysteries of Christ as necessary for
a return to God.

"I believe that this is the main reason why our invisible God
desired to be seen in the flesh and took on human features so
as to be able to speak to men; He took into consideration that
creatures of flesh unable to love except with an earthly love
(that is of the flesh) would long with all their heart for the

saving love of His flesh. Thus, they would gradually discover a spiritual love."[66]

The one who has come to the knowledge of revelation *(communicatio)* and has been drawn into the process of *conformatio* is led by Bernard to the *recordatio,* the *commemoratio,* the *memoria* of the mysteries of Christ, all of which are sources of *devotio* and *affectio.* "These things are constantly on my lips . . . I have them constantly in my heart," Bernard says of himself about the life but above all about the passion of Christ.[67] For this reason he can write: "I do not see Christ as accessible only to my prayers but I dare even to imitate Him." For Bernard, the imitation of Christ is given birth in the *recordatio* and *devotio.*

To this introductory statement we must add a second: imitation together with the whole of a virtuous life and the ascetic combat, as also the remembrance of the mysteries of Christ and the devotion it engenders will be brought together and specified by growth in love, by a progressive transition from a love that is carnal to a love that is spiritual. Bernard explains this using the example of Christ's humanity: "Even though an attachment to the body of Christ is a very great gift of the Holy Spirit, I call such a love still carnal when compared to the other love which does not have as its object only the Word made flesh but the Word as Wisdom, Justice, Truth, Holiness Piety, Virtue and other such titles. For Christ is all of these together . . ."[68]

Therefore, one must speak of a progressive passage from a carnal to a spiritual imitation of Christ. This transition is brought about through a spiritualization of one's contemplation of the mysteries of Christ. Bernard addresses himself chiefly to this in his writings and sermons; rarely does he treat of different spiritual degrees of imitation of Christ (except in his two works on humility and the love of God). Frequently, whenever the imitation of Christ appears, it is not developed at any great length for its own sake but is presented as a natural consequence of knowledge and love; it is in effect the fruit: "There is no argument more powerful than the imitation of Christ to give evidence that His passion and His likeness to us have borne fruit in our souls."[69] Bernard even arrives at the point where he speaks as if the imitation of Christ were the goal where one's faith is verified: "(Jesus) gives Himself as an example of humility and a model of gentleness. If we imitate Him we do not walk in darkness but have the light of Life . . . When finally I believed in Christ, that is to say when I imitated His humility, I came to know Truth."[70]

Furthermore, as A. Van Den Bosch has pointed out,[71] Bernard presents the imitation of Christ at times as that which conforms the Christian to the likeness of Christ, as that which makes one a truly living member of the body of Christ and which gives expression to God dwelling in him. It is a matter then of imitation, in spiritual love, of God become imitable in Jesus, that is, of the God whose inner mystery of Goodness is made known to us in the humility of Jesus, and not a matter only of the humility that is the fruit of a true knowledge of oneself.[72] Philosophers have come to the knowledge of God's majesty and the Jews to a knowledge of His power. But "power demands submission and majesty calls forth admiration; neither of these lead to imitation. Show us then, Lord Jesus, your goodness, so that man created to your own image might imitate you for we are unable to imitate and we ought not to envy your majesty, your power and your wisdom."[73] This then is the reason for the incarnation: "Might acts for me, likeness acts for me, but only if there is imitation by which I follow in His footsteps."[74] Without the Word incarnate, "it would be impossible to rediscover anywhere in this world the likeness" that has been lost. But this is now possible to us because of Christ.

"Being the splendor of His glory, the perfect image of His substance and upholding all things by His Word, He appeared endowed with all that is necessary to effectively reform what was deformed, strengthen what was weak and render it wise, dispelling the darkness of sin by the radiance of His face and strengthening us against the tryranny of the devil by the power of His word."[75] Thus man "freed from sin will begin to recover the liberty that comes with wisdom and regain his rightful place by regaining his true likeness to the image of God which he bears within himself and which is even being reestablished in its original beauty." A generous and joyous effort will enable him to "imitate in all things the divine Wisdom."[76] Still, however, he has need of "the help of Him who urges us on by His ex-

ample since it is He who alone can conform us to this wisdom
and transform us into His own likeness . . . by the breath of the
Spirit of the Lord."[77]

2. St. Francis of Assisi (†1226)

In the few writings of St. Francis and in the accounts left to
us by his brothers, what is most striking is the constant reference to the gospel which more precisely means: the life of the
Man-Jesus who is God. "Blessed is the religious," he says to
his brothers, "who finds pleasure and joy only in the holy words
and actions of our Lord and uses them to bring the love of God
to men with great joy."[78]

E. Longpré has already given us the spiritual itinerary and
the doctrine of St. Francis;[79] we will limit ourselves to relating
the theme of imitation of Christ to this synthesis. It is important that this relationship be situated within the synthesis to
which we refer.

a) The word which Francis of Assisi seems to love best
to express the evangelical ideal by which he intends to live and
have his brothers live in the word "follow." He uses it at least
eleven times, whereas the word *example* is used only once and
the word *imitate* is never used (except in the later title of
Counsels 6), nor is the invitation in Philippians "to put on
Christ." "To follow Christ" is the phrase Francis found in the
Synoptic gospels: three texts are quoted at the beginning of
the first chapter to his first Rule (Mt 19:21 and 16:24; Lk
14:26). He also freely uses 1 Pt 2:21 which he quotes in his
letter "to all the faithful," addressed no doubt to all those Christians drawn to the ideal of Francis.

"The will of the Father was that His blessed and glorious Son
whom He gave to us should offer Himself in His own blood as
a sacrifice and victim on the altar of the cross; not for His
own sake, for all things were made by Him, but for our sins,
leaving us an example that we might follow in His footsteps."[80]

The phrase "follow in the footsteps of Jesus" appears four
times: twice without further elaboration[81] and twice with a
kind of addition, one which points to the doctrine of our Lord,
"follow the doctrine and footsteps of the Lord,"[82] and one to
poverty, "follow His footsteps and poverty."[83]

Other complementary additions to the verb *sequi* indicate what we are to follow. One must follow the will of the Lord and please Him;[84] the humility and poverty of the Lord;[85] the life and poverty of the Lord,[86] and also the good Shepherd in His sufferings and in His death.[87]

The words and example of Jesus are to determine the manner of being and acting of the brothers whether it is concerned with their personal behavior or their interactions among themselves or with others. Eight prescriptions are justified with the words of Jesus.[88] The example of Jesus is as evident as are His words: the fast in the desert,[89] the life of poverty and almsgiving,[90] the manner of preaching briefly,[91] persecutions encountered,[92] the kindness toward Judas,[93] the washing of the feet,[94] the Cross,[95] and in general His love on which our own must be patterned.[96]

If Jesus is the good Shepherd, it is that we might share His lot. This is the theme of the 6th counsel to which editors readily give the title "Imitation of the Lord": "Consider, brothers, the good Shepherd who suffered the shame of the cross for the salvation of His flock. These have followed after Him in His sufferings, His persecutions, His humiliations, in hunger and thirst, in weakness and trials, etc. In return they received eternal life from the Lord. We should be ashamed, we who are the servants of God. For the saints so acted ..."[97] Such is the ideal directly revealed by the Most High,[98] which inspired the whole of Francis' life.

b) Those who were witnesses to the life of Saint Francis allow us to perceive how he lived out these teachings. They also testify to the truth of the image Christianity has given us of this saint. The oldest sources like the *First Life* of Thomas de Celano (1228), collections of later composition like the *Conformity of Blessed Francis' Life with that of the Lord Jesus* by Barthalomew of Pisa written around 1385 and the *Fioretti* which date from the end of the fourteenth century depict Francis primarily as he who followed the Lord and was conformed to Him even in concrete circumstances.

Francis takes literally the demands of the words of Jesus. When he heard, for example, the command given by Christ to the apostles to have neither gold, nor silver, nor wallet, nor staff (Mt 10:7-14), he shed at the door of the church his hermit's cloak, his shoes and his staff, his wallet and belt and put on an old rag tied at the waist with a rope.[99] He even relived certain scenes from the gospel such as when on the night of Easter he walked as an unknown pilgrim to the convent of Greccio.[100]

He sought to do what Jesus did when, for example, considering the discourse of Christ, he sent his brothers on mission, two by two, or when he refused a cell built for him because "the Lord had neither house nor cell built for Him."[101] But Thomas of Celano does not see an intention to imitate Jesus in Francis' desire to be laid out naked on the naked earth at the moment of his death. The saint still feared the demon and wished "to combat naked the naked adversary."[102] The gift of the stigmata of Christ's passion imprinted in his flesh could only be interpreted as an evident configuration to the death of Jesus.[103]

A hundred other facts and stories which illustrate the teachings of Francis and their realization in his life explain why his contemporaries spontaneously gave him the title of imitator of Christ. Gregory IX in his proclamation of canonization said: "Francis was conformed to Him who, rich though He was, became poor for our sake."[104]

Saint Clare called him "the imitator of the poverty and humility of the Son of God and of the glorious Virgin, His Mother."[105] For her "the Son of God has become the way which was pointed out to us and taught to us both in word and example by our blessed father, Francis, this true lover and imitator of Christ."[106] Thomas of Celano sees him "a most holy mirror of the holiness of our Lord and an image of His perfection,"[107] and indicates that the love of the dying Francis for his brothers makes him truly the imitator of Christ his God.[108]

Pius XI echoes a constant tradition when he writes: "No one seems to have existed in whom the likeness and pattern of Christ's life were more striking and more radiant than in Francis. Also, he who called himself the herald of the great King has been rightfully called another Christ."[109]

c) Does the word "imitation" surpass the expression *sequela Christi* ("following of Christ") and is it in greater correspondence to the intention of Francis of Assisi? It would, doubtless, be imprudent to overstress the opposition. For Francis, who was not a pilgrim to the Holy Land, the *vestigia Domini* ("traces of the Lord") are to be found in the gospel, in what our Lord said and did, in His manner of living and being, in His virtues. And if He is the way we are to follow to go to the Father, is it not right to let His way of living flow into our own life? One text in the Rule which invites the brothers to mutual service and obedience is thus justified: "Such is the true and holy obedience of Our Lord Jesus Christ."[110]

Some have seen in this imitation nothing but a complacency in suffering and abjection, or a rigid literalism. It is true that in Francis there is an asceticism, a detachment, and abnegation which is pushed to its ultimate and which takes the gospel literally. But we must remember the place the crucified Christ had in his life from the time of his vision at Saint Damien to that of Alverno.

Whatever might be Francis' attraction for the Passion and the humanity of Jesus, he declares condemned "those who see in Our Lord Jesus Christ only His humanity,"[111] and he reaches out toward the glory where Christ awaits his elect,[112] with a mentality that could be called eschatological.

Literal imitation is different from literalistic imitation. Francis is so open to all forms of imitation that he writes to brother Leo: "Whatever way seems best for you to please our Lord God and follow in His footsteps and His poverty, adopt it with the blessing of our Lord God and my permission."[113]

It is in the depths of his faith that one must try to understand Francis' tenderness for Christ's humanity, his passion to imitate Jesus Christ, to "follow" His life and especially His humility, His poverty and His obedience. E. Longpré has shown well that what holds first place for Francis is adherence to Christ: Word incarnate, Christ crucified, Christ always living in the Eucharist and in the Word of God. It is from this adherence to Christ that flow devotion to the Virgin, loving fidelity to the Church and the Franciscan virtues of poverty, humility, obedience, penance, and austerity. It is from this adherence that his mystical life springs forth and culminates with the stigmatism at Alverno.[114]

3. St. Bonaventure (†1274)[115]

4. St. Thomas Aquinas (†1274)

In the works of Saint Thomas Aquinas the theme of imitation of Christ is presently particularly in his biblical commentaries which are indeed rich.[116] The importance of devotion to the humanity of Christ in the 14th and 15th centuries has already been shown,[117] so we will not return to it.

D. The Sixteenth and Seventeenth Centuries

1. St. Ignatius of Loyola (†1556)

The spirituality of service to Christ in His body which is the Church as understood by St. Ignatius has already been presented.[118] The Christ of Ignatian spirituality must be seen as the Mediator, the Commander, the perfect Servant of the Father and in this perspective as the Model proposed for the imitation of one who wishes to follow and be "with Him." On the other hand, the "mysteries" of the human life of Christ as presented to us in the gospel and which the *Exercises* develop for our meditation give standards of choice (actions, spiritual attitudes) for the one who wishes to "follow," to "imitate" Christ, "to come to Him."[119]

2. Cardinal Bérulle (†1629)

A study of the imitation of Christ in the French spiritual writers of the 17th century would demand long research and many pages. But a special place must be found for the doctrine of Pierre de Bérulle whose influence was extensive on men like the Oratorians, on J.-J. Olier (†1657) and the Sulpicians, on Saint John Eudes (†1680) and on priestly spirituality. We know that between 1922 and 1929 a discussion arose between H. Bremond and F. Cavallera[120] in which Bérulle's concept of adherence was opposed to Ignatius' concept of imitation. Bremond considered the latter as directly depending on asceticism and the former as clearly mystical.

There is no question of studying here Bérulle's notion of adherence.[121] The vocabulary of Bérulle evolved, as did his thought, particularly about the motive for the Incarnation, a very important question from the viewpoint of the imitation of Christ. We will simply seek to establish that Bérulle's spirituality implies the idea of imitation and calls it forth, with or without using the word.

Bérulle was "the apostle of the Word incarnate." For him a return to God is possible only because of Jesus Christ. "There is an infinite distance between the divine nature and human nature and it would be so forever if Love, as powerful and as infinite as nature, did not unite so intimately the divine nature to human nature."[122]

Jesus is the perfect worshipper "loving, adoring and serving the supreme Majesty in a way that is worthy of its being loved, served and honored . . . O greatness of the mystery of the incarnation to establish an infinite condition and dignity within our created being."[123]

This infinite adoration is rendered to the Father by the Word incarnate, fundamentally, in that His humanity has no personal subsistence since it is totally related to the person of the Word just as the eternal Son is but a total relation to the Father. In this absence of personal subsistence, the humanity of the Word is at once both abased and magnificently exalted, "deified," as Bérulle so often puts it. There is here a "holy and sacred bond" which united the humanity of Christ to the person of the Word, "a bond which creates a new being, a new condition, a new order."[124] From now on the best adoration, the only true adoration possible, will be for man also to annihilate himself as does the eternal Son: "As the Son of God, by right of subsistence, is in possession of the human nature which He has united to His person, so do I want Jesus by the right of a special and particular power to condescend to take possession of my spirit, of my condition, of my life, and that I be but a naked capacity and pure emptiness in myself."[125]

This desire becomes a prayer: "O my Lord Jesus, grant that I may live and subsist in you as you live and subsist in one divine person! Be my all and may I become part of you in your mystical body as your humanity is part of a divinely structured subsistence of two so very different natures."[126]

The humanity of Christ, in effect, is always operative. The mysteries of Christ "are over as far as their accomplishment but they continue to be present by their virtue and their virtue never passes away, nor will the love with which they were accomplished ever pass away. The spirit then, the state, the virtue, the merit of the mystery is always present. The Spirit of God by which this mystery took place, the interior disposition of the external mystery, the efficacy and the virtue which make the mystery living and operative in us, this state of virtuous disposition ... is always alive, actual and present in Jesus."[127]

We have only to adhere to these mysteries, refer to them, aspire to possess them, bind ourselves to them, appropriate them to ourselves. And this is true whether it is concerning the mystery of the Word incarnate in as general a vision as we can have of it, or concerning the particular mysteries of the life of Jesus which are like the economy or the dispensation of the substance of the one unique mystery. The method is simple. Bérulle describes it many times, for example, in relation to the three captivities of Jesus: in His infancy, in His sufferings and in the Eucharist.

We know that abnegation holds a dominant place in Bérulle's spirituality.[128] This abasement is chosen for the purpose of sharing in that of Jesus Christ. The *Manual of Direction for Superiors* which uses the word *adherence* to Christ five times on one page to express the disposition necessary for those who desire to direct souls also says that humility is a "worthy foundation for the science of salvation and the school of the Son of God who hid His power and His wisdom in the humility of His infancy and of His cross."[129] All of this indicates a call to imitation: "Offer to our Lord Jesus and to His most holy Mother, in honor of the weariness of the Cross, your soul, your labors and the beginnings of this house."[130] Certainly for Bérulle as for every Christian, speaking more profoundly and more mystically than other writers, "this imitation will be but the result of a collaboration in which Christ Himself has the leading role,"[131] but the thought of imitating Christ cannot be put aside. "Adherence culminates in imitation."[132] "It goes without saying that this adherence urges us on to imitation. Having in us the sentiments of the Word incarnate, we desire to act as did the Word incarnate in whom the Spirit is never at rest."[133]

Bérulle does not fear the word. From contemplation, it is normal to pass on to imitation. There are three uses, he writes in 1623, to be made of the gift of the Word incarnate: elevation, dependence and reference.

"In these three usages and different ways of looking at Jesus Christ, our Lord, we have the principal obligations of the religious life. You are hosts immolated to Jesus as He is a host immolated to God, hosts of praise, of thanksgiving, and of love. You must be in relationship to Jesus as He is in relationship to His Father; attentive to Him as He is to His Father; dependent on Him as He is on His Father; seeking His glory as constantly as He sought His Father's glory; and Jesus, your life, must always be before your eyes in order to live out this imitation and this complete conformity with Him."[134]

For the one who adheres to Christ and has entered into His dispositions, everything becomes matter for imitation of Christ. "There are some saintly souls . . . the more they are filled with God, the more they love Him and the more they experience and see their indigence in relation to Him . . . This is a great thing and a way of interior suffering which is high and elevated, the work of God in the depths of the soul, a way which first began in Jesus Christ on the Cross."[135]

"The Spirit of God calls the way of saintly souls who tend toward him a course . . . after the example of Him who, not being content simply to come to us, chose to come in stride, 'like a giant running his course,' that is Our Lord Jesus Christ. Imitate Him in His ways, contemplate Him in His mysteries, invoke Him in your miseries."[136]

The spirituality of adherence has been expressed by Bérulle in many ways. In abstract terms: renounce one's own personal subsistence and have none but that of Christ. In quasi-juridical terms in texts which are concerned with the vow of service: to honor the abasement of the Word incarnate and His destitution even to death on the cross, to divest oneself of all autonomy, to make an oblation of all that we can be in the order of nature and of grace, to consecrate one's life to serve "not only by vows and actions but also by a way of being and a condition which binds me and orientates me to you in a unique rapport so that as you are always mine, I am always yours and that there is in me a permanent quality which gives you perpetual honor and homage."[137] Finally, adherence can be expressed if not in its root at least by its expected fruits, in the simple and traditional forms of imitation: "You must find in Him (Christ incarnate) a new life, imitating His pilgrim existence so that He will make you worthy to participate in it, that is to say, that your acts of virtue be a participation in the spirit with which Our Lord accomplished His."[138]

3. Jesuit Spiritual Authors

Jesuit spiritual writers of France in the 17th century certainly welcomed other influences besides that of St. Ignatius. We know that Bremond made of some of them "Bérullian Jesuits."[139] It is certain that their Christocentrism and their conception of the role and place of the imitation of Christ is particularly brought into relief by the doctrine of Jesuit works written prior to Bérulle: that of Jacques Alvarez de Paz (†1620),[140] of Antoine Le Gaudier (†1622)[141] and of Pierre Coton (†1626),[142] whom we know introduced the influence of Gagliardi into France.[143]

a) Without going into the sources he used, we present the doctrine of the imitation of Christ taught by one who is habitually considered as the leading man in a long line of French Jesuit spiritual writers: Louis Lallemant (†1635). Lallemant has a unique esteem for the interior life and for prayer. He insists greatly on docility to the Holy Spirit which could be termed passive: "When a soul is abandoned to the guidance of the Holy Spirit, little by little the inner light illumines it and enables it to see all its actions and God's providence in its actions in such a way that it has little else to do but to let God do in it and through it what pleases Him; and so it advances marvelously."[144]

Lallemant gives an equally important place to the practice of the virtues and to the imitation of Jesus Christ. When he speaks of recollection and the interior life, he concludes by indicating the best way to practice the virtues: "One must simply try to recognize which virtues God wishes us to put into practice in each action and then simply fulfill this action in the presence of God with the intention He inspires in us and motivated by the desire to imitate Our Lord. This is the reason why we so highly recommend the love of Our Lord, which can motivate us easily, which is accessible to everyone, and which is filled with gentleness. And the good that we do according to the principle of this love—an act of temperance for example which

we practice in order to imitate Our Lord and to please Him—
such an act is far more excellent than one which is done simply
to maintain the moderation prescribed by temperance."[145]

Then there follows immediately the "principle" of union with
Our Lord: "the soul unites itself to Our Lord in three ways:
by knowledge, by love and by imitation."[146] Here is the essential reason for this imitation: "Jesus Christ wants us to be His
images as He is the image of God His Father, not only because
He is God but also because He is man; and just as the perfections of God radiate in His blessed humanity, He desires
that we radiate in our conduct His own spirit and His gifts so
that by a perfect expression of these virtues we become like
Him. The acts of virtues which we perform motivated by the
desire to imitate Our Lord and resemble Him are nobler and
more agreeable to God than those which we perform motivated by the desire to be virtuous."[147]

Six chapters are devoted to explaining in what ways we are
to imitate Jesus Christ: in separation from all creatures, in His
poverty, in His chastity, in His obedience, in His humility, and
in His interior life. If the first five instances are a matter of
moral virtues, Lallemant shows how they have their model in
Jesus Christ. The Word incarnate was detached from all things
to the extent that "in His mortal life He received from creatures
only pain and sorrow." How then can we be attached to
creatures?[148] He took on poverty by taking on our human nature
and lived it in all the circumstances of His life.[149] In His eternal
generation and in His temporal generation He is infinitely pure.
"We ought to celebrate continually the nuptial feast of the divine
union of our souls with Jesus Christ."[150] Jesus Christ obeyed
perfectly the will of His Father, being obedient for us even
unto death.[151] The measure of Our Lord's humility is the abasement by which the Word humbled Himself becoming man.
Jesus Christ in His blessed humanity, seeing the abasement of
the Word, abased Himself because of this example in all possible ways and especially in the Eucharist, "and in desiring only
lowliness, abjection, poverty, labor, and trials" which are the
lot of our creatureliness.[152] If there is in this some mystical
aspect, i.e. the nuptials between Christ and the soul and the
abasement of the Word, it is in general to the moral virtues of
Christ that Lallemant refers our own virtue; and this is of

capital importance, for they are never presented as having value in themselves: poverty has value only because Christ willed to be poor; it is the same with all the other virtues.

The chapter on the imitation of Christ in His interior life is very short. In Christ "it consists in his attachment to God, in His attitude, His understandings, in His love, in His zeal and desires which were infinite to such an extent that we can say that all that He did and all that He suffered exteriorly is as nothing compared to what went on within Him. To urge us on to imitate Him in this, we should presume as most certain, that all our perfection depends on the interior life." But Lallemant does not explicitly compare our views and our sentiments to those of Christ. He is content to justify his assertion with three reasons. The interior life helps us to live the theological virtues, the noblest of the moral virtues (religion and penance), and the most perfect of the gifts of the Holy Spirit (wisdom, understanding, and knowledge). Through the interior life, God acts in us: "Sometimes He gives us in prayer greater gifts and greater help than we could acquire in several years of exterior actions even of zeal and charity."[153]

On the other hand, the chapter on the usefulness of the mystery of the incarnation for perfection returns to the ascetical concept of imitation. "In the Incarnation we find new reasons to incite us to the love and the practice of the moral virtues; for, since God become man practiced them, they have an excellence and a beauty which they did not previously possess. They are as it were deified in the person of Jesus Christ. Besides He taught us many virtues which we did not know or that we knew only a little, like humility, poverty and love of enemies. A God-man is the most noble, the most perfect and the most appealing model that men could ever propose to themselves."[154]

b) It would be fitting to study also the spiritual descendants of Lallemant. We will mention only a few.[154a] Suffice it to recall something that applies to them as it does to the vast majority of French spiritual persons of the 17th century: their doctrine of the imitation of Christ can never be isolated from the spiritual conformity and the union of the interior Christian to Christ.

E. The Eighteenth Century

1. Writings on the Imitation of Christ

The 18th century was prolific in religious works. Even if there were fewer outstanding spiritual persons than in the preceding century, the literature on spirituality and piety did not diminish. For our theme one would need to look at vast numbers of manuals or Christian handbooks, pamphlets of devotion, spiritual retreats, etc.[155] We will refer here to a few works which pertain directly to the imitation of Christ,[156] then mention three Italian saints who addressed themselves to this theme.

2. Three Italian Saints

a) Leonard of Port-Maurice (†1751)

Leonard of Port-Maurice is a preacher who possessed a fervent devotion toward Christ; if his sermons address themselves primarily to the moral life, it is one that is dominated and held in tension by the personality of Christ, His greatness, His beauty, His goodness, and the example of His love even unto death. The principal devotions preached by the saintly Franciscan are: the way of the cross, devotion to the Sacred Heart, and adoration of the Blessed Sacrament. The imitation of Christ is to be found mainly in his devotional pamphlets. *The Way of Paradise,* which was well known in Italy, often speaks of Christ's example: "To imitate Jesus in our actions is to love Him truly."

b) St. Paul of the Cross (†1775)

St. Paul of the Cross is the best known mystic of the period. His notes and letters when first read do not seem to express the imitation of Christ as much as the will of God, abandonment, and mystical participation in the Passion. M. Viller points out with the help of texts how this imitation of Christ is intimately related to participation in the Passion.[157] S. Breton does the same using the *Retreat Journals* of the saint[158] in his book *Mystique de la Passion.*[159]

c) St. Alphonsus de Ligouri (†1787)

Saint Alphonsus de Liguori[160] is a missionary, a spiritual

writer and founder of a religious community who is more like
Leonard of Port-Maurice than Paul of the Cross. The Re-
deemer-Christ is the way to God the Father. The Christian
and especially the priest and religious are vowed to the imitation of the life and virtues of the Saviour. Numerous texts
scattered throughout the enormous output of the saint verify
this. A good example of his style is given in *The Practice of the
Love of Jesus Christ*.[161]

F. Charles de Foucauld

From the 19th century up to the present time, the history of
Christian life gives evidence that this life means centering more
and more on attachment to the Person of Jesus. "To imitate
Christ, to follow Him, to be conformed to Him, to cling to Him,
to live as He did and with Him—these are the recurring aspirations in the spiritual writings of the century, in retreats, preaching, and devotional practices."[162] This commentary on the 19th
century in France could be extended to the whole Catholic
world of that time.

We choose to study only one person, but a significant one
whose influence has become important in our day. Charles de
Foucauld is important not because his spiritual doctrine is
particularly new or well elaborated but because his personal
life is a manifestation of what it means to love and follow
Jesus Christ.

Charles de Foucauld (†1916), later known as brother
Charles of Jesus,[163] has given us the best of himself in a selec-
tion of gospel texts which he called *The Unique Model* (Marseilles, 1935). A letter which he wrote to Abbé Henri Huvelin
in 1906[164] enables us to determine that it was written around
1898 and that Foucauld entertained the idea of publishing it.
The title is significant as is the gospel text used as a subtitle:
"The servant is not greater than his Master; he is perfect if he
is like his Master . . . Follow me!" Except for one page which
presents "the goals" of Jesus and a resumé of His life, the content of the book is "the principal virtues taught" by Him. The
words of Jesus, what He said about Himself, about His Father,
the Spirit, our vocation, all follow one another without apparent order, mixed up with examples which he himself gives and
stresses. The whole gives us a portrait of the Jesus who capti-

vated Charles de Foucauld and a portrait of the Christian like Jesus whom the convert of Abbé Huvelin sought with fervent humility to realize in himself.

All of Foucauld's writings are a witness to this. "Jesus Christ so truly took the last place that no one can snatch it from Him." These words spoken to him by Abbé Huvelin became the keynote of his life. He sought in his own way to take the lowest place among the men of his time because it was there that he would be nearest to Christ."[165] So he decided to join the Trappists: "I didn't know what order to choose: the gospel told me that the first commandment is to love God with all my heart and that all I did was to be done out of love. We know that love leads to imitation; there was nothing else for me to do except to enter the order in which I would find the most perfect imitation of Jesus."[166]

But is the Trappist life truly the best form of imitation of Jesus? Foucauld asks himself "if it would not be better to look for a small group with whom one could form a little community whose purpose would be to live as nearly as possible the way Jesus lived . . . following to the letter all of the counsels, possessing nothing, giving to whoever asks . . . so as to be like Jesus."[167]

After much hesitation, Foucauld accepted the priesthood as a deepening of his desire to imitate Christ: "The priest imitates more perfectly Our Lord, the sovereign Priest, who offers himself daily. I must be humble as Our Lord was, put humility into practice as He did and do so as a priest following His example."[168] If the thought of martyrdom haunts Foucauld it is because it is the best way to achieve total identification with Christ.

There are certainly many ways to imitate Christ according to one's particular vocation and there are many ways individual Christians can hear God's call: Foucauld's slow ascent to the priesthood and experience with various forms of life is evidence of this.[169] But the imitation of Christ remains the constant of his Christian life; the priest and the hermit of the Sahara which Charles de Foucauld later became tell of the same desire that burned in the Trappist of Our Lady of the Snows or the yard man of the Poor Clares in Nazareth. It is to imitate Jesus Christ that Foucauld gave his life, that he desired to be hidden in Jesus the Poor One, that he sought to bring Jesus the Saviour to the world.[170]

Charles de Foucauld wants to share with others his ambitious desire to imitate Christ and this primarily with those with whom he lives: "The imitation of the hidden life of our Lord Jesus at Nazareth, together with perpetual adoration of the Blessed Sacrament and a burning love for others, are the principal characteristics of the Little Brothers of the Sacred Heart of Jesus."[171]

A letter to the Poor Clares at Nazareth specifies how to live such a life of imitation: "In order to be entirely detached from yourself, to forget oneself totally and to be concerned in all things with God's glory, the best way seems to be to ask yourself constantly what Jesus would think, say, or do in your place and then to think, say, and do what He would do. In this way you will forget yourself completely since your one desire is to imitate Jesus and so you will be concerned not with yourself but with the glory of God, since you live like Jesus who lived only for this glory. May Jesus help you to imitate Him . . . That is why He came to dwell among us, so that we might always have an easy way, available to all, to practice perfection: we have only to look at Him and do as He does . . . To look at, to imitate, to obey Him—and in this way to unite ourselves to Him in love by becoming one with Him through the loss of our own will into His."[172] It would not be difficult to multiply texts of this kind. They are as abundant in his notebooks as in his correspondence.

Although Foucauld studied theology and was interested in the lives of Jesus and commentaries on the gospel, he does not refer to these explicitly in his spirituality. Must we then look for the influence of the French school which inspired Abbé Huvelin or of the *Exercises* of St. Ignatius which he made at Clamart in 1889, or of St. Francis of Assisi whom he came to know through the Poor Clares and the Third Order? It seems that Foucauld's spirituality is one of pure and simple imitation of Jesus. He met Christ. He knew himself loved and wanted to love in return. This is evident beyond discussion. One final text bears this out.

"The simplest and best means to unite ourselves to the head of our Spouse is to act, speak and think always and in all things as He did, remaining in His presence and imitating Him. . . . In all that we do, say or think we should ask ourselves . . . how did He do it, say it, think it; in like circumstances what would He do, say, or think in my place? . . . Jesus himself taught His disciples this method of simple union with Him. . . : 'Come and see' . . . Come, that is to say, 'Follow me, come with me, walk in my footsteps, imitate me, do as I do'; See, that is to say, 'Look at me, remain in my presence, contemplate me.' . . . Presence of God, of Jesus, and imitation of Jesus . . . all perfection is in this . . . It is clear as day that he who does as Jesus does is perfect . . . Let us then enter with our whole being into this divine imitation . . . and let us look at the Beloved One . . . He who loves loses and plunges himself in the contemplation of the Being who is Love."[173]

"Be united . . . Imitate." The bond between these words is constant in Foucauld. It is his most basic intuition: "If anyone was united to Our Lord surely he was. But what path does he recommend to arrive at this desired union? Only one: love which is put to the test, love pressed even to the practical and active imitation of Jesus Christ. Those who do not go this far are in some way lacking in their love."[174]

Chapter III

Theological Reflections

by Pierre Adnés, S.J.

In order to have a clear idea of the imitation of Christ, we must first of all clarify the meaning of imitation in general from a strictly human viewpoint. We can then understand better what imitation of Christ has that is both particular and specific.

A. Imitation in Human Life

The Latin verb *imitari* derived from *imago* signifies: to seek to reproduce an image. To imitate is to act, either consciously or unconsciously, to do or strive to do the same thing that another does, to take that one as a model, to follow his example.

Modern psychologists and sociologists have shown the important role played by the conscious or unconscious phenomena of imitation in the mental and social development of an individual. The psychic evolution of the child from this point of view has been the subject of numerous studies. Some sociologists even believe that it is through imitation that social life comes into being. Operative at all levels of the personality, imitation could explain how psychic realities pass over from the individual to the inter-individual sphere: human society is simply an ensemble of individuals who imitate one another. This is the thesis developed by G. Tarde.[1] The thesis appears to be something of an exaggeration. "Imitation conditions social life, it does not constitute it."[2] We should not, however, underestimate its importance.

"The influence of imitation in human life is immense. For the most part education, in the most general sense of the word, that is, the assimilation by a child or a person of manners of acting, of feeling, of thinking in his milieu, the development of techniques, of language, of needs, of beliefs, of all the cultural elements sustained by tradition, all of these rest on imitation."[3]

What is of direct interest to us is the place which certain modern philosophers give to imitation in the moral sphere of life. In this respect, the phenomenological analyses of Max Scheler (†1928) are of great interest. Scheler distinguishes the chief from the model. The chief acts by way of authority or of command and it is in the mode of obedience that, in principle, another reacts to his influence. The concept of model is quite different. The "model," in the profound sense of the word, always implies value. He acts by way of example or by the radiating power of his personality. He does not impose the value but it comes alive and attractive through him. Those who follow him react to his influence with an attitude of imitation *(Nachfolge),* which must not be understood in the sense of copying or reproducing in a material way *(Nachahmung).* A chief addresses himself only to our will. A model fashions our very being. Scheller defines the model as "the value incarnated in a person, an ideal figure which is constantly present to the soul of the individual or the group, so much so that little by little, the traits of that person are acquired and are transformed into oneself: one's being, one's life, one's acts, consciously or unconsciously, are ruled by it in a way that causes the subject to be pleased with following the model or to reproach himself if it is not imitated."[4]

There exists of course a "deliberate" fidelity towards a model, a fidelity that is personally conscious of itself as well as of the nature and implication of the influence received. But Scheler concentrates on describing a kind of "vital" fidelity which is mysteriously imprinted on the soul and which can escape the distinct perception and at times the consciousness of the soul that is influenced.

"The person (or the group) who follows a model need not know the model in a conscious way or be aware that he has such a model, nor that day by day he shapes his very being on the other, fashions his personality on his. I would go even so far as to affirm that the person rarely knows the model as an ideal whose strong character could be defined, and that he knows even less to the extent that the formative action is more powerful."[5]

The "disciple," at any rate, does not obey the power of suggestion which emanates from the model. Nor does he copy the model. But while remaining himself, without however remaining the same, he experiences that the originating force of his own action is no longer within himself. His response to the obligation he experiences is lived as an "attraction" *(Zug)* created by the model. As it develops and becomes more precise, the attraction becomes love. This love is not concerned with this or that characteristic or action of the model, but with the very heart of his being, his spiritual essence, in which he now participates. In this form, the relationship of fidelity is apt to effect a moral transformation in the disciple, a conversion of his spirit, a renewal of his being which neither obedience nor respect for abstract norms could possibly bring about. It is in the radiant beauty of real persons, in the example which shapes our very lives that we must first of all find the origin and stimulus for moral progress and not primarily in the formal rules of universal application.

In different terms, Henri Bergson (†1941) comes to a similar conclusion when he opposes a morality that is narrow and grounded on the general imperatives of impersonal formulas to a morality that is open, incarnated in a "privileged personality who becomes for us an example," and draws us in a contagious, persuasive manner, to "a common imitation of the model." "Why do the saints have so many followers and what have great men that draws crowds after them? They ask for nothing and yet much is given to them. They have no need to exhort; they have only to be. Their very existence is a call."[6]

But a personalist philosophy, which considers imitation to be a primary source of moral conduct, encounters a difficulty. If my primary obligation is to become who I am, to discern and fulfill the task reserved for me alone and which no one can fulfill for me, is it not strange that in order to fulfill it I must act at the instigation of another person and conform myself to someone who necessarily holds in the moral order a position different from mine? Scheler responds by saying we are neither slavishly to copy the person-model nor become who he is. What is operating in us is essentially a modification or, more precisely, a conversion of the condition of our spirit under the influence of the person-model. We become imbued with the spirit of our model without this fact deciding our actions or what expression our spirit should take. In this way we will learn to desire and to act *in the manner* in which the model desires and acts, but not desire what he desires, nor do what he does.

While recognizing that the influence of a model constitutes one of the privileged modes of action of man on man, other authors denounce in a way that is clearer than Scheler the dangers and illusions of imitation when it is misunderstood. Georges Gusdorf writes: "The model . . . does not impose a pattern to be followed trait by trait. The temptation to a literal and slavish reproduction represents in fact the worst form of influence. Such influence tends to deny the very mission it has of drawing to oneself only in order to liberate." Models usually present us with certain values subject to historical perspectives different from our own. They can serve to inspire us, to guide us in the choices and adventures which are not their own. But they must remain a means to bring about the realization of one's own personal life which is each one's task. "Every man bears his own law within himself and any influences received from without can be for him only indications and signs on the road to his own development."[7]

For his part, Edmond Barbotin comments that imitation risks introducing us into rigid types and conventions which are no longer those of an authentic moral existence: "The imitation of moral conduct cannot but release the amoral forces of mimicry. This is especially true in communal life where the example of a great person easily loses its value and becomes conformity and is moral only in appearance. In reality, the uprightness of moral action demands much more than an exact reduplication of the model; rather it calls for the personal acceptance of the moral intention, the interiorization of the spiritual motivation, the creation of a personal response to a call whose value is ever unique and ever new."[8]

B. Imitation in Christian Spirituality

When it is a question of Christ, imitation takes on a quite different character. The danger would be to reduce the imitation of Christ to the simple categories of ethics as if it did not differ in nature but only in degree, from the imitation provoked by great men of goodness and the radiating personalities of great religious figures. Even if certain of the preceding analyses can help us to understand what the imitation of Christ is, let it be understood that it signifies much more, something infinitely more profound than imitation that is purely human, no matter how perfect it might be. It is impossible to speak of the imitation of Christ in purely phenomenological terms because Christ Himself in His person and in His actions transcends the basic givens that are within our reach and the laws which we can formulate about phenomenology. Let us say at least that the imitation of Christ realizes and fulfills in an eminently superior way the very concept of imitation.

1. Christ as Model

Christianity is adherence not to an abstract law and to commandments but above all to *a person* who is "the way, the truth and the life" (Jn 14:6). From this point of view, a certain personalist ethic is easily applicable to Christian spirituality, if it is not this very spirituality which first brings it into being.

Christ is not only a saint, a genius, a hero, and an exemplary figure whose contagious power of persuasion overwhelms us. He is, for Christian faith, *the Son of God,* the Word incarnate. What is seen in Him is not only a certain typical grouping of values, but God Himself, the Absolute. "He who sees me, sees Him who sent me" (Jn 12:45). "He who sees me, sees the Father" (14:9). His humanity is the sacrament of God. Also, the divine-human person of Christ cannot be recognized for what it truly is except in faith and by faith, a faith that is not only a human confidence like that which we can have in certain exceptional personalities, but a supernatural faith which is beyond man's power and which is a gift of God. "No one can come to me unless the Father who sent me draws him" (Jn 6:44). This attraction, this call, is essentially the work of grace. Christ is not only God revealing Himself, giving Himself;

He is God instructing us. Before being a model for us, Christ is *the Master* who "has the words of eternal life" (Jn 6:68), and who "teaches as one having authority" (Mt 7:29). This authority claims the obedience of man. To follow Christ is above all to do what He commands. Without doubt, as Master, He demands obedience only by first making visible in His person the value of what He commands. But it can also happen that the disciple is unable as yet to grasp clearly this value. He still has the duty to obey. His obedience, nevertheless, is not blind. He knows that everything commanded by Christ is good, simply because it is He who commands it. Values are values only in God. They can represent an obligation for us only because they are imposed on us by God.

While being Master, Christ is also *Saviour*. The salvation given us in Christ is not only salvation on an ethical plan, a conversion to the order of values which makes known to us our own personal, interior law and which will enable us to find ourselves. It is a salvation which uproots us from the grasp of sin and bestows upon us a new life, a divine life. And it is by His death and resurrection that Christ obtained this for us, He who was "put to death for our trespasses and raised for our justification" (Rom 4:25). This salvific action of Christ is the principal motive of the Christian's love for Christ. This love is not simply an attachment to an ideal personality who has impressed us, but a response of love to the greatest love that is possible, that which lays down its life for its friends (Jn 15:13). "He loved me and gave himself for me" (Gal 2:20).

We must add that for the faith, obedience, and love of the Christian, Christ is not a personality of the past. He was admittedly born in Palestine, lived there, taught, and suffered at a determined time. The gospels, without being exactly a "life" of Jesus and, without always satisfying our curiosity, report or at least let us glimpse certain episodes and aspects of His historical existence. But Christ triumphed over death. His tomb is empty. The Christian need not "seek Him who is the living one among the dead" (Lk 24:5). The risen Christ is a living person, "the Living One" par excellence, who lives "forever and ever" (Rev 1:17-18). We cannot have for Christ the same attitude that we have for a great historical figure to whom we have access only in memory or in writings concerning him.

Much more, because Christ is a divine-human person who by His most profound reality transcends time, the facts of His earthly existence which are past in their historical reality are always present in their spiritual reality, in their interior dimension which is expressed in their efficacious and salvific power. In some way it is today that Christ is born, dies and rises as the Fathers of the Church have said. The "mysteries" of Christ are always "actual." Christ is truly contemporary to every person.

These considerations enable us to conclude that the imitation of Christ must necessarily assume a particular form. It cannot be simply a type of psychological imitation. Anyone who would wish to take Christ as a model in a purely human way would bypass a truly Christian imitation of Christ. He would not even discover its threshold.

2. The Characteristics of the Imitation of Christ

This imitation is fundamentally *sacramental.* Through the specific sacrament of entry into Christian life, the Christian imitates and follows Jesus in the event of His redemptive death. He dies to sin "by a death like unto His" and obtains "by a like resurrection" a participation in the life of the Risen Christ (Rom 6:1-11). He becomes "a new creature" (2 Cor 5:17), "a new man" (Eph 2:15), a member of the mystical Body of Christ animated by the Spirit (1 Cor 12:13). Baptized in Christ, he has "put on Christ" (Gal 3:27). It is a question of radical transformation which can be termed ontological. This transformation is brought to perfection by the Eucharist which enables the faithful to participate mystically in the sacrifice, resurrection, and ascension of the Lord. By receiving the Eucharist, food and nourishment of this new life, the Christian unites himself intimately to Christ glorified and with Him is transformed and exalted. This is what is meant by the traditional affirmation: "The Eucharist is a spiritual nourishment which is not transformed into the one who receives it but transforms the one who receives it into itself." Baptism and the Eucharist make real then the sacramental imitation of Christ, bring it about, create between Christians and Christ a community of being and of destiny which fulfills the divine plan of salvation, the mystery of God's will, by which He "destined us in love to be His sons through Jesus Christ" (Eph 1:5), "predestined to be conformed to the image of His Son" (Rom 8:29). It is the task of the Christian life to develop and bring to perfection unceasingly this basic conformity with Christ which will not be complete until the end of time. But because it is above all a gift of God, it is by His grace that it must grow.

We touch here on another characteristic of the imitation of Christ. It is in us, principally, the *work of the Holy Spirit.* This Spirit, given to us in Baptism and who is the very Spirit of Christ (Rom 8:9; Phil 1:19; Gal 4:6), enables Christ to dwell in the heart of the believer (Eph 3:16). In this way the model is not external to the one who must imitate Him. In last analysis, Christ becomes in a way the subject of all the vital actions of a Christian. Such a one can say with Paul "It is no longer I who live but Christ who lives in me" (Gal 2:20). It is this Spirit, dynamic principle of life and action, grace uncreated and sanctifying, who makes us desire to resemble Christ always more, who reproduces ineffably His traits in our soul, who fashions us according to His image. It is not by accident that Paul's teaching on the imitation of Christ is characterized by certain virtues which the apostle presents elsewhere as the fruits of the Spirit.

There is a final aspect of the imitation of Christ on which we usually insist very little but which is very important. It is the *ecclesial* character of this imitation. It is primarily through the Church that we come to know Christ. She is herself the sacrament of Christ as He is of the Father. Her mission is to present Christ to us for our imitation. She presents Him to us in the preaching of the Word of God whose central object He is, in the administration of the sacraments of faith which make His redemptive work a reality, in the unfolding of the liturgy which helps us to contemplate His mysteries throughout the year. Truly, the Church alone possesses and preserves the integral and authentic image of Christ our model. Outside the Church this image is often retouched, diminished, deformed. It tends to vanish. The imitation of Christ must rest solidly upon a theology of the incarnation which is genuinely orthodox.

The Christological controversies, which are the origin of the formulation of dogmas, from Nestorianism and Monophysiticism to Monothelism, are not just scholastic wrestling matches. To be our model, Christ must be fully human; but this model would not be divinely efficacious if Christ were not truly God. It is also the Church who guarantees the fidelity and the validity of our imitation of Christ and preserves it from hazardous and erroneous interpretation. The Christian who is serious about his conformity to Christ must compare the subjective image which is being formed in him to the objective image offered by the Church. He is assured that any discrepancy between his image and that of the Church will have for its author not the Spirit of Christ, but his own spirit.

3. *Ways and Degrees of the Imitation of Christ*

The transformation effected by the sacraments, the interior action of the Holy Spirit and the external action of the Church, which complement each other without contradicting each other, does not dispense the Christian from bringing his active cooperation to the task of conforming himself to Christ. Quite the contrary, this effort of conformity can have many various degrees depending on the special vocation and grace given to each "according to the measure of God's gift." (Eph 4:7).

There is the first degree which is content to submit the disciple's activity to the law of the Master. It is the docility of pure obedience in which one does not perhaps entrust entirely the depths of his being to the control of Christ and which could be considered as quite external but nevertheless very precious. To follow Christ, as was said earlier, consists essentially in this: to obey Him because He is the Master who makes known to us the will of God. We must not harbor any illusions. This first degree is the foundation of everything. And it goes far. For the law of Christ is very demanding.

The second degree is that spoken of by St. Paul to the Philippians (2:5): "Have this mind among yourselves which was in Christ Jesus *(Hoc sentite in vobis quod et in Christo Jesu)*." This is a more interior conformity which takes in the whole person even to his affectivity, and is born of a desire for an intimate communion of "person to person" with the Lord. The adoption of Christ's sentiments towards God, his neighbor, and himself ends with the Christian's becoming another Christ *(Christianus alter Christus)*. It demands humility and obedience to the will of the Father like Christ's own kenosis (Phil 2:1-11); renouncement of one's own interests and of certain rights in imitation of Christ who "did not seek to please Himself" (Rom 15:3); faithful patience in accepting unjust trials, even persecution, in keeping with the example of Christ suffering (1 Pt 2:18-25; 3:13-22); the spirit of service, for Christ came not to be served but to serve (Mt 20:28); generosity to the poor because Christ, "rich though He was, became poor for us" (2 Cor 8:8-9); love of others even to the sacrifice of one's own life, like Christ who gave His life for those whom He loved (Jn 13:34; 15:12-13; 1 Jn 3:16), etc. This degree is within the reach of every Christian, whatever his condition, his professional responsibilities or family background. But it is susceptible to being pressed even further. Some will embrace voluntary poverty and freely chosen celibacy in order to better resemble the poor and chaste Christ.[9]

At any rate, the imitation of Christ is never for the Christian simply an external conformity to an example, an unintelligent copying. It is not a matter of doing the same physical gestures Christ did. Christ does not want copies but disciples. Even at the scene of the washing of the feet, it is not the action itself that Christ recommends but the spiritual attitude which this gesture implies (Jn 13:14). It is thus that the Church has understood it from the beginning. Only the fundamental attitudes which animate Christ can and must be in some way the model for Christians. In this way imitation escapes being mimicry. The Christian must aspire to a form of conduct conformed to Christ's, a conduct imbued with His spirit and sustained by the large vision which He had. To want to copy Christ would be an illusion and even an injury to the unique stature of the Master; it would be a matter of being unconscious of the inaccessible character and absolute uniqueness of Christ both in His person and in His destiny.

Certainly we find saints who have imitated Christ even in ways that appear to us quite literal, like St. Bernard and St. Francis of Assisi. Closer to our own times, there is Charles de Foucauld who put great emphasis on the external imitation of the hidden life of Jesus of Nazareth. But this literal imitation is not "literalistic" because it was truly the spirit of Christ that they sought to assimilate through the literal imitation. And maybe it is necessary at certain times to have persons who practice this type of imitation to arouse the dulled consciousness of other Christians.

4. Means of Imitating Christ

We do not seek what we do not know. Conformity to Christ presupposes a knowledge of the person and actions of Christ. This knowledge is the first means to imitate Him. It is to be sought first of all and quite naturally in meditation on the gospel. We know the place such meditation has had in Christian piety beginning with the Middle Ages, sometimes naively, as can be seen in the *Meditations on the life of Christ* attributed to St. Bonaventure or *The Life of Christ* by Ludolph the Carthusian.[10] Such meditation is not so much intellectual as affective contemplation on the gospel texts with which the Christian nourishes his thoughts, his imagination, and his heart in order to transform his life according to the image of Christ. It is this contemplation of the heart which St. Francis de Sales (†1622) describes: "By looking often at Our Lord in meditation, your whole soul will be filled with Him. You will learn the features of His face and the form of your actions will take on His... Children, by listening to their mothers, stammering along with them, gradually learn their language; and we by remaining near our Saviour by meditation, by observing His words, His actions, His ways of loving, will learn with the help of His grace to do and to will as He does."[11]

But instead of taking our point of departure in the contemplation of the earthly life and action of Christ, we can, using a perspective that is probably more in accord with St. Paul, begin with the reasoned contemplation of the Word incarnate in His mysteries. This is also in accord with Bérulle. The mysteries, in their spiritual sense, are facts in the life of our Saviour which, although they are past events and actions, are still actual insofar as we consider the inner motivation and perpetual disposition of the God-Man. They have the power to communicate to the soul the image of Christ because they contain for us not only a lesson but a secret power and efficacy, a particular grace which varies according to their diversity.

"This obliges us," wrote Cardinal Bérulle (†1629), "to treat the mysteries of Jesus not as events that are past and over but as things living and present and even eternal from which we can gather fruit that is both present and eternal."[12] Addressing himself to the Word incarnate, he says: "May I adore you, may I contemplate you in this life, in these conditions and in these mysteries, may I bear the traits and effects which they can have and imprint on me, may their grace and power be applied to me!"[13]

A very simple and fruitful manner of coming to know and contemplate the mysteries of Christ is to follow the Church's liturgy which unfolds for us each year the complete cycle of the mysteries of Christ. This point of view is developed by Columba Marmion (†1923).

"Man can imitate in two ways the example of Christ. He can attempt to do it by a work that is quite natural as when he attempts to reproduce a human ideal presented by a hero or a person he admires... This is to lose sight of the fact that Christ is a *divine* model...Only the Holy Spirit, 'Finger of the Father's Right Hand,' is able to reproduce in us the true image of the Son because our imitation must be in the supernatural order. And so this work of the divine artist is best done in prayer rooted in faith and grounded in love. While, with the eyes of our faith and a love which desires to give itself, we contemplate (in the unfolding of the liturgical year) the mysteries of Christ, the Holy Spirit who is the Spirit of Christ is intimately active in the soul and, by His sovereignly efficacious touch, molds the soul in a way that reproduces in her, as by a sacramental virtue, the traits of the divine model."[14]

It is certain that contemplative and liturgical prayer is a very sure way to be assimilated to Christ. It produces a kind of living assimilation. One becomes what one contemplates. But it is also evident that this way does not exclude the effort of the Christian to model his virtues and actions on those of Christ. This then is the second way to be conformed to Christ. It is, moreover, not a purely natural way. This effort of man is itself a gift of grace. It is artificial to oppose two schools of spirituality: one which would advise the Chiristian to let grace operate in him and transform him into the image of Christ; the other which would suggest that he strive generously to reform himself in the likeness of the divine model. The two aspects complement each other and are mutually fulfilling.

It is no less artificial to oppose the tradition proper to the

East defined as "a life in Christ," to a tradition characteristic of the West which seeks a conformity to Christ by imitation.[15] In fact, it is possible that the westerner, more inclined to action, has often understood conformity to Christ in an ascetical and moral sense rather than an ontological and mystical sense. However, there is no need to choose. It is because the Christian lives in Christ and Christ lives in him that he becomes able to imitate Him by constant spiritual effort. And the consequence of this effort is a more intimate union, a deeper identification with Christ. In this way "Christ is formed in us" (Gal 4:19) and we "grow up in Him" (Eph 4:15).

5. Situating the Imitation of Christ

Beginning with St. Thomas Aquinas, the theme of imitating Christ is abandoned by moral theology and left to pastoral theology and then to ascetical spirituality. This imitation becomes the characteristic of the illuminative way "so called because it consists mainly in imitating Our Lord by the positive practice of the Christian virtues, where those making progress are to be found."[16] But new orientations tend to find a place for the imitation of Christ in moral theology.[17]

Stating the theory of his position, Haring writes: "The fundamental concept of Christian morality is uniquely that of *imitation*. In it is found, without any possibility of misunderstanding, all that makes Christian morality a morality that is truly religious and truly Christian. It is not a principle, it is not an idea, but it is Christ who is our faith. Imitation as well as a loving attachment of obedience to Him is our morality."[18]

It is not for us here to say if we can reduce Christian morality to one of imitation and include all of its detailed ethical demands under one heading. But what is to be thought of spiritualities which do not insist on imitation of Christ nor make explicit allusion to it and seem to be structured in an altogether different frame of reference? We can answer by saying that it is not the word that matters. All Christians desire and consider themselves as disciples of Christ, and intend in some way to walk in His footsteps. But this concept of walking in His footsteps contains implicitly that of imitation. "For what is it to follow Him except to imitate Him?" said St. Augustine.[19] On the other hand, as Scheler points out, in order to be influenced by a model, it is not necessary to know him in a reflective way or to consciously want to imitate him. The radiant person of Christ is necessarily present in the faith and love of the Christian. According to the measure of this faith and love, it cannot but exercise on him its formative action, whether he thinks of it or not, and imprint on him the characteristics of its image and fashion him in his sentiments and in the depths of his spiritual being.

Chapter IV

The Imitation of Christ
in Daily Life

by Aimé Solignac, S.J.

"What I am now doing is trying to *incarnate Christ*. Often it happens that in difficult moments I find myself saying: *What would Christ do?* And immediately I understand."[1] Taken from among many others, this witness of an 18-year-old boy is significant. He situates the imitation of Christ in the sacrifice of self. He understands it as an effort to "relive" Christ in the present situation. He will serve then as guide in this presentation.

A. Imitation of Christ: Norm of Christian Living

Christian existence is not defined in terms of a moral code or ethical values; the *vita christiana* is specified by the person of Christ. It is a life patterned on the example of Christ, with Christ, for Christ, "in Christ," as St. Paul never tires of saying. We are not unaware of the obstacles or the screens which modern culture (demythologization, hermeneutics, "God is dead" theology, etc.) interposes between the man of today and the Person of Jesus Christ. We will not attempt here to resolve these difficulties nor to situate them in their proper context. The exegetical presentation has shown that it is advisable to narrow the distance between the "Jesus of faith" and the "Jesus of history," that the invitation to "follow Christ" was not intended solely for the disciples or the "professionals" in the apostolate.[2] A "Christian life without Christ" is an endeavour without hope as well as a contradiction in terms.

The imitation of Christ is the response of man, his responsible cooperation with the design of the Father to "conform those whom He had chosen to the image of His Son, that he might be the first-born among many brethren" (Rom 8:29). This design is of primary importance and in this sense Luther's formulation quoted above remains true.[3] Every Christian *is* then by divine design and *should become* by free choice "another Christ": *Christianus alter Christus.* Assimilation to Christ is consequently the fundamental aspect of holiness to which all are called. It is the universal vocation which is at the heart of all personal or special vocations and endows them with value. The holiness and also the spiritual radiance of a priest or of a religious is not to be measured by institutional conformity to Christ's functions and way of life but by existential assimilation to His Person, His attitudes and His actions.

B. Imitation of Christ Diversified according to Personalities

In the last analysis, each Christian bears an original, unique and incommunicable aspect of Christ's personality. It is his *personal vocation* which is related to the "charism" received for the edification of the Body of Christ and which urges him on to express some aspect of Christ's Person or to situate himself in some particular moment of Christ's existence. Thus Charles de Foucauld pursued the impossible dream of grasping from Christ "the last place." The "country priest" of Bernanos— who is more than simply a literary figure—finds his place near Christ in the agony of Gethsemani.

On the other hand, one can also say that each Christian, in the Church as the "Pleroma" (Fullness: Eph 1:23), *completes* in his own way the body of Christ whose full expression remained incomplete during the time of His earthly existence: "Jesus of Nazareth in His limited and too brief career was unable to give His full measure . . . He who is 'Man' par excellence, that is, in possession of all human perfection and is the model of all men, was unable to live in a single limited existence all of the various forms of human experience . . . All the canonized saints and all good Christians without official halos will be needed in order that the perfection of God made man, which is dazzling but always more or less known or unknown, might conquer the darkness little by little."[4] Each Christian reveals but one feature of Christ and is at the same time for Christ "an added humanity." Such is the mystery of the Body of Christ.

The imitation of Christ does not achieve in each person the same degree of perfection. The average Christian who is content to follow the commandments of God in general and the teachings of the gospel and is grieved that he doesn't succeed, imitates Christ to some extent even if he is not concerned with referring his existence to the person of the Saviour. It is not necessary that the imitation be conscious and willed; it is necessary and sufficient that it be real. There have always been simple persons whose education consists in the depth of their faith and the quality of their love, and who follow Christ in His trusting submission to the will of His Father and His concern for people. Such persons do not fall into empty conformity and legalism for they go far beyond prescribed obligations. These persons of faith and of love bear a witness more powerful than the greatest sermon. Others deliberately commit themselves to crying out "the gospel in all of their life," to making the gospel "the charter of their existence." Individually or in groups by a sharing of the gospel, the revision of life, or in other such ways, they try to discern and fulfill the design God has in mind for men and for the world. In this way, they continue the work of the Saviour and, guided by His example, they live "their present life by faith in the Son of God who loved them and gave Himself up for them" (Gal 2:20).

Furthermore, the imitation of Christ which coincides with the realization of the *image of God* in man, follows a path of gradual progression. The child educates his freedom by obeying the example of Christ who submitted himself to Mary and Joseph. The adolescent, like Jesus, strives to grow "in wisdom and grace before God and man" (Lk 2:52). The adult places himself at the service of others because "the Son of man came not to be served but to serve" (Mt 20:28). In like manner, in the beginnings of a life of prayer, meditation on the gospel leads to resolutions inspired by the acts or words of Christ. But the law of progress in the spiritual life is intended to lead us from the external to the interior by penetrating our entire personality with the "sentiments" (Phil 2:5) of Christ so as to conform our actions to His. St. Ignatius asks his retreatants who are as yet unaccustomed to prayer to petition for an "interior knowledge of Jesus Christ ... so as to love Him better and *follow Him*."[5] Interior knowledge, love and the "following" of Christ go together, and are purified and enriched together, throughout the various stages of the spiritual life. In the end, the mystic shares in some way the intimacy of Christ with His Father and can say with Him: "All that is mine is yours and, all that is yours is mine" (Jn 17:10). If he no longer needs to refer explicitly to Christ's humanity, this is because through purification and the grace of interior illumination, he has been rooted in conformity to Jesus Christ.

C. *To Imitate Christ: "Incarnate Christ"* by *"Doing what Christ Would Do"*

The task of the Christian is not to read the gospel but to live it, or better still, in the challenging words of John XXIII, "to bring the modern world into contact with the vivifying, perennial, and divine energies of the gospel."[6]

At first, imitation tends to look *to the past,* to the existence of Christ in history but it is *in the present* that it must be lived so as to become a discernible and actual sign of His presence and action in the world today. In the midst of the needs, cries and aspirations of all peoples, the Christian must try to understand what form and what method can best achieve the design of God for the human community and for the world in our time and then he must work to bring it about. And far from putting limits on his intelligence and liberty, the imitation of Christ, on the contrary, challenges his highest potential for discernment, invention, and creativity. For this reason, the reading of the gospel and the example of Christ need to be enlightened by the Holy Spirit and the teaching of the Church which this same Spirit animates. The conciliar documents of Vatican II, the encyclicals of John XXIII and Paul VI, the doctrinal and pastoral directives of the episcopal conferences, etc., must be taken into consideration as indicative norms of the ways by which the Christian must be actively committed if he would "incarnate Christ" today according to the measure of his gifts and talents. It is evident that this imitation of Christ cannot be achieved by the single, individual person; it is the mission and work of the entire Church and calls for an ecclesial actualization.

D. To Imitate Christ: Live Out His Fundamental Attitude of Love

In its essentials, the example of Christ can be expressed in the twofold unity of His love of the Father and His love of people, of love and of sacrifice. The "will of the Father" which is the expression of His love, is His desire to "give His only Son" so that all might "obtain life eternal" (Jn 3:16) and receive "the power to become children of God" (1:12). Christ is in perfect communion with this will of His Father and he "gives His life" both out of love for the Father (14:30; see 10:17) and out of love for us (1:11; 11:51-52, etc.). Christ's sacrifice in His human existence which he lived at the heart of a sinful world is the very expression of the complete and absolute return which the Son in His eternal existence accomplishes in relationship to the Father at the heart of the Trinitarian mystery.

Christ gives us no commandment except one which is an expression of His own existence: "Love one another, as I have loved you; greater love has no man than this, that a man lay down his life for his friends" (Jn 15:12-13). The love of the Father is not explicitly referred to because it is included in "as I have loved you." Christ calls *new* (13:34) this commandment which places the highest demands on our imitation and states that it is *His* (15:12). Lived in community, it will be the *sign* by which His true disciples will be known (13:35). What distinguishes the person who is "specifically Christian" is a love of the Father and a love of people which is lived in a profound unity of intention with Christ and with the readiness to sacrifice himself even to death if necessary. The acceptance of sacrifice is a verification of the authenticity of love; reciprocally, love leads to joy in its communion with the mystery of the death and resurrection of Christ (16:20-22).

This love is therefore the *form* of the Christian life. It is useful, however, to specify this form into a *structure* which will help us to determine the demands made by the imitation of

Christ. Several complementary and eventually equivalent structures could be considered, beginning, for example, with the Beatitudes and the Sermon on the Mount, the parables, the teachings on renunciation, poverty, chastity. Or again, one could begin with the epistles of St. Paul and of St. Peter. The parenetic section in the Letter to the Ephesians, a charter of Christian life, offers without doubt the most complete synthesis: the diversity and complementarity of charisms "for building up the body of Christ" (4:12-13); purity and holiness demanded of those who "have learned Christ" (4:20); truth, concord and decency in relationships, mutual goodwill, "as God has forgiven us in Christ" (5:32); the gift of self and concern for mutual perfection in conjugal love in imitation of the love Christ has for His Church (5:25); respect for persons in parent-child, master-servant relationships (6:1-9); and finally, the necessity of spiritual combat and of prayer (6:19-18). We do not arrive naturally at Christian love. This love has constant need to be purified by the struggle against the powers of evil and the complicity they find in our very nature. As St. Ignatius put it, we achieve a love able to "commit itself and distinguish itself in unstinted service" only by "struggling against a love that is carnal and worldly" (*Exercises,* n. 97).

To imitate Christ is man's greatest vocation; it is also the most difficult. Nevertheless, we must resolutely say—and not only to escape the suspicion of Pelagianism—that it would be impossible to actualize this imitation if we were left to our own resources. But the Christian is the person who is transformed by the new life "of water and the Spirit" (Jn 3:5), nourished by the Bread of Life which enables him to live because of Christ as Christ lives because of the Father (6:57), led by the Spirit who enables him to "act as a child of God" (Rom 8:14), and assisted by the teaching and fraternal support he receives in the Church. And so the ultimate goal of Christian existence is made accessible to us without ceasing to be paradoxical: "Therefore be imitators of God, as beloved children. And walk in love, as Christ loved us and gave Himself up for us, a fragrant offering and sacrifice to God" (Eph 5:1-2).

Chapter V

A New Look
at an Old Classic

by Bernard Spaapen, S.J.

A. *General Character of the* Imitation of Christ.[1]

According to the adage which seems to go back to Saint Augustine and which is cited in the *Imitation* (I, 5, 1), "It is for truth, not for literary excellence, that we go to the Holy Scripture; every passage of it ought to be read in the light of that inspiration which produced it." One may, without doubt, by extension, call the *Imitation* a "sacred writing." From this point on, the *incipit* and the actual title set us immediately on the way. We know in fact that the first chapter of the first book starts out with the quotation from Jn 8:12: "He who follows me will not walk in darkness." As in a number of other examples from the Middle Ages, this *incipit* furnishes the title not only of the first book, but also of the entire work. The latter is then from the very beginning placed under the sign of the "following of Christ." The *sequela Christi* is moreover the subject of the first chapter; it urges the Christian to imitate the life and the virtues of Christ (I, 1, 1), to adopt His spirit through meditation upon His doctrine (2), to conform our existence to His (2). The imitation, the following of Christ, is the major theme of the work, upon which the author is going to develop his reflections in the course of the four books. What is proposed for the reader's imitation lies not so much in examples of the concrete life of the Lord—these are mentioned only incidentally—as in his spirit (I, 1, 2). The author does not present this spirit in a methodical teaching, theologically synthesized, such as will be produced two centuries later by the masters of the French School. He seeks rather to cause it to penetrate into us as he himself has without doubt been penetrated by it: through reflection upon Holy Scripture, and through consideration of the examples of the Saints, the Christian assimilates and incorporates little by little the spirit of Christ into the tissue of his own existence.

This spirit of Christ the *Imitation* vigorously opposes to fallen human nature. It invites man to fight against the disordered demands of his nature in order to allow himself to be impregnated by those sentiments which were Christ's. "You must make room for Christ" (II, 2). To submit human nature marked by sin to the purifying and transforming grace of Christ in order to make of this nature a new creature is, it seems, what constitutes the ultimate goal of the imitation, of the following of Christ, the heart and the overall plan of the entire work.

Therein too lies its distinction from the numberless collections of wise sayings composed by the sages of humanity. The *Imitation* has not the depth or the breadth of view of the *Tao Te King;* the ascesis which it proposes lacks the technical and psychological perfection of the *Aphorisms* of Patanjali; its humanism does not attain to that of an Epictetus or of a Marcus Aurelius. But what distinguishes the *Imitation* from other masterpieces of human wisdom, what confers upon it its own value, is that it introduces man into that mystery which is inaccessible to any psychological technique or to any natural contemplation: the mystery of the person of Christ, who is at once Man and God. In line with the spiritual traditions which it crowns, it puts the soul into communication with and soon into life-giving communion with the spirit and the grace of Christ, and thus it introduces man into closeness with Him who is the Origin and the End of all life.

On the other hand, the *Imitation of Christ* does not demand on the part of its reader any heavy intellectual baggage. It is addressed equally to the highest intelligence and to the man of little learning. It speaks not so much to reason as to the heart and thereby to the fine point of the spirit. This book which proceeds from the heart ought to be received into the heart. Or again one might say that it communicates a spirit and through this spirit a life, rather than teaching first of all a doctrine.

We touch here upon a final point which is important to note: the *Imitation* was born of the practice of the spiritual life; it yields its secret only to one who sets himself to this practice, however sinful he may be. The man who seeks to know the truth of his being, who desires to be liberated from the powers of evil and to be formed to the image and likeness of God, finds in these pages an access to the grace and spirit of Christ. He receives from them a certain interior understanding and experience of the reality of the peace, the presence, the consolation of Christ, the interior liberty of the Christian, the love of charity. He enters thus into the experience of the spiritual life at the same time that he enters into the heritage promised to the sons of God.

B. Author

The author of the *Imitation* is a priest and very probably a cloistered monk (see III, 10, 2). All his energies are directed towards the interior life; the edification of the Church, the spread of the Gospel hold very little place in his work and do not appear to be his major cares, whence we may suppose that his form of life is that of a monk rather than that of a canon. He is a contemplative before all else and lives in the desire for God; this desire readily finds its place in the current of interior piety which has its source several centuries before him and flows through the whole of medieval Christianity. The piety, the interior spirit, the docility, the seeking after simplicity, which characterize this spiritual current, contrast singularly with the rational demands and the analytical complexity of the scholastic spirit, which comes after him.

In the mind of the author, the essential task for mankind *in via* is to tend towards the union of love with God. He is persuaded of the powerlessness, even the uselessness of reason before the mystery of a transcendent God. Hence he scorns the vain speculations of the Schools. He knows that the shortest path to a grasp of the mystery of God is through the mystery of man; he reenters therefore into himself. In this movement he seeks to separate himself from appearances, from the unreal, the false, the counterfeit, all that is not important, and to establish himself in the true, the real, the essential, what is important.

This search for the true and eternal center of man ceaselessly recommenced day after day finally leads to an attitude of humble expectation of the grace of contemplation, of interior consolation. The author manifests in his book a vital need, as it were, of this experience of grace, because it is for him a sign of God; he can doubtless do without this experience; however, leaning on the memory of graces already received, he longs for those which will yet be given for the support of his weakness as a man who is a sinner.

C. Literary Genre

The *Imitation* is a book belonging to a particular genre; we must find out what this is, for otherwise we shall not be able to estimate it at its proper value. We are not dealing with a single work divided into four parts, but with four distinct books composed at certain intervals of time, which are like moments in one and the same intellectual and spiritual development. We note that the affective tone is increasingly accented from book to book. These books are collections of thoughts, designed to awaken and to nourish the interior life of man. The truths which they enfold have not been arranged according to a precise play, a rational structure, or a psychological dialectic.

Attempts to fix in some systematic order the texts of the *Imitation* have resulted in failure. Dissected, the book loses all life, and we perceive that in fact its doctrine neither pretends to, nor lends itself to, systematization. Hence it is at least imprudent to say that the first three books represent the threefold purgative, illuminative, and unitive way. This does not prevent the *Imitation* from being a work of spirituality: it simply presents, not a systematically elaborated theory, but a doctrine which springs from a lived experience.

One of the great attractions of the work consists precisely in its simplicity, in its "authenticity." However, although it abounds with psychological observations and although the author shows an exceptional knowledge of men, we cannot attach it to the genre of the intimate journal or the personal notes

of a soul on the way to perfection. The *Imitation* is certainly
the very personal work of its author, but thanks to the literary
process, and thanks especially to the aphoristic genre, the
individual experience is sufficiently veiled, softened in outline
to permit the reader to approach it with a sense of ease and
to remake it, if only partially, according to his own manner.
On the other hand, it is quickly apparent that the personal experience which informs the whole of the *Imitation* is entirely
related to the traditional teaching of the Church, to that of
medieval spirituality, but above all to Scripture. The author
truly awakens its interior sense in the reading of the Bible,
from which he draws thoughts and maxims which guide and
enlighten him in his journey towards perfection. The choice
which he makes of Bible texts is judicious. He adapts them
with sovereign discretion to his diverse spiritual states. We
appreciate how profoundly the author has been able to conform
his spirit to the spirit of Scripture; the proof of this is that his
thoughts often appear to be only adaptations or applications of
texts of the Bible.

Can we place the *Imitation* among the *rapiaria?*[2] Without
excluding all connection with this sort of writing, a connection which we shall need to consider more closely later on, we
cannot answer this question positively. In the first place, the
Imitation is not uniquely or even principally a collection of
extracts from the Bible or from spiritual authors, such as monks
of the early Middle Ages or representatives of the *Devotio
Moderna* loved to compose. Although borrowings made from
writers of this tradition are not lacking, it seems to us however
that, apart from Sacred Scripture, on which the author has
drawn in such large measure, the substance of the book is
formed from personal thoughts. Then, the spirit which guided
the author of the *Imitation* is clearly apparent: he did not
wish to prepare an anthology of various authors on definite
and well ordered themes, according to a fully determined doctrine of perfection, as did for example Florent Radewijns in
his *rapiarium "Omnes, inquit, artes,"* (All the Arts, He says).[3]
The author of the *Imitation* utilizes his sources in a quite different manner. He brings them into the current of his own
thought and makes them serve his own ends. He has assimilated them with such extraordinary suppleness and liberty that

we succeed only with great difficulty in distinguishing them, so completely have they lost the mark of their origin. This is true even for the first book, which perhaps bears the closest resemblance to the genre of the *rapiaria.*

What then is the book's position in relation to this literary genre? The author, it might be said, has followed the method of composition of the *rapiaria,* by arranging in a certain order and under the form of maxims texts either born of his own thought or found elsewhere. Nevertheless, just as an artist passes beyond the academic rules even while he makes use of them, he has raised himself above the narrow conventions of the genre in order to create a completely original work.

The author has then formulated his thoughts under the form of *maxims,* which confers upon them a character of concision and clarity which most of the translations try to preserve. These apothegms, although each one is sufficient to itself and may be detached from the others, mutually reenforce and clarify one another. Their force of expression is further increased by the fact that they have been refined by verbal processes, such as assonance and rhyme.

A very personal writer, the author of the *Imitation* shows a mastery of thought and style which is strengthened from book to book. What he lacks perhaps is the relaxed tone which one remarks for example in the writings of Saint Bernard, or of that other master of the maxim, Guigues I the Carthusian.[4] Contrary to those spirits who were able to keep themselves hidden in the background with regard to what they experienced, the author of the *Imitation* was unable to release himself so completely from the grip of his experiences, and that marks his style with a character sometimes tight, sometimes even heavy.

D. Sources

To list the sources which the author of the *Imitation* has utilized is a difficult matter. Not only do we lack a comprehensive study, but even the soundings which have been made on this question leave a double impression. To begin with, the author has so completely assimilated his sources that they appear to be amalgamated with his own thought; then the work which he has left is much more personal and autonomous than has previously been supposed.

With the exception of some pagan authors, such as Ovid, Aristotle, and Seneca, whose few sentences are reported almost word for word, textual quotations are rare.

Rare, too, are the texts which may be traced with certainty to one of the Fathers, such as Augustine, Gregory the Great, Bernard, or Bonaventure. The influence which the last named probably exercised on the *Imitation* seems less great than has been claimed. Similarity of ideas has been noted with Ludolph the Carthusian, John of Dambach, and particularly with Henry Suso. It is probable that the author borrowed certain themes from the *Monks' Mirror* of David of Augsburg. There have also been noted certain parallels of ideas with John Ruysbroeck, Henry Egher de Kalkar, John of Schoonhoven, Gerard Groote, and numerous other writers of the *Devotio Moderna*.

However, there is one source, by far the most important, which patient study has succeeded in bringing to light almost entirely: Holy Scripture. The *Imitation* has woven into it more than a thousand quotations from the Bible. The books most often quoted are the Psalms (140 times, notably the Penitential Psalms), the Wisdom books (60 times), the Prophets (42 times), Job (24 times), etc. In the New Testament, Saint Paul is utilized more than the four Evangelists (120 times against 100).

Many expressions might correspond to texts quoted more or less freely; but here we have conjecture rather than certitude. However this may be, it seems more desirable to possess some day a good complete study on the influences exerted upon the author of the *Imitation* than to succeed merely in establishing an exhaustive list of textual quotations and free quotations.

E. Major Themes

If the *Imitation* is not a continuous treatise developing a systematic doctrine, we can none the less discover it in a certain number of themes to which the author returns apparently spontaneously, which he completes and enriches with successive touches in favor of his meditations, readings, and experience. Such are, for example, the themes of the vanity of the world, the misery of material goods, false happiness, self-love, unregulated affections, temptations, the danger of intellectual pride; all things from which we must be detached. Also included are the goods of the Kingdom of Heaven, such as peace of heart, interior liberty, purification of the senses and of the spirit, abandonment without reserve to God, patience, obedience, and frequent Communion. Access by the Christian to these goods of the Kingdom supposes above all humility, compunction of heart, simplicity. In various places throughout the *Imitation,* the author lays bare the movements of nature and of grace. In contrast to the authors of the *rapiaria,* who are too exclusively moralistic, he loves to expatiate on grace and on the experience which it is given to us to have of it, on the happiness of union with God, on love and devotion, in brief on the spiritual life, but with an insistence on its affective aspect. All these fundamental themes are dominated and oriented by the figure of Christ, who is to be imitated and followed. Taken thus in their ensemble and subordinated to the Person of Christ, these main lines of the *Imitation* establish a spiritual teaching, trace a spiritual way. Certain themes, however, have more particularly marked one or another of the books.

F. General View of the Four Books

Each book of the *Imitation* has its own physiognomy, which it is the purpose of the following notes to set in relief.

1. The First Book

The First Book has for subtitle: "Practical Advice About the Spiritual Life." It has as its purpose to develop the interior man, the true man; it teaches, therefore, aversion for all that is exterior, banal, illusory, false, and it invites the soul to set about seeking and watching out for what is interior, true, essential. Man must tend, then, to keep himself at the center of his being and, with this view, to turn his attention away from what passes outside of himself in order to fix it upon the truth of his own existence. It is useful to emphasize here the connection between this doctrine of the *Imitation* and the fundamental goal of existential philosophy. It is a question of liberating the soul in order that it may appear to itself such as it is in its depths, that it may live according its noblest and most radical penchant: its tendency towards God.

For this interior liberation, the author does not lead either through an esoteric teaching or through the exacting techniques of psychological control, but through that way at once human and divine which is Jesus Christ, a way which He has traced and which the Saints have followed after Him, and which is possible to every man. It is the way of Christian interiorization: all that distracts man from his truth, and therefore from God, all that tends to disperse his powers among exterior things is vanity. Thus the *Imitation* considers as vanities not only superfluous conversations, useless goings and comings, aimless wanderings outside of the convent, and all the dissipations of psychological awareness, but also, and even especially, that unregulated search after knowledge, whether profane or theological, which causes men to "put knowledge first, instead of conduct" (I, 3, 4).

"To put conduct first" becomes possible only if, in habitual recollection, one comes to know, through assiduous contemplation as well as through a generous and faithful practice, the price and the fruitfulness of Christian *virtue*. The *Imitation* presents this virtue neither so much as a mastery of self and a knowledge of how to act, nor as a guard which keeps man from going astray after his passions, but rather as a manner of being and living according to Christ, a manner in which is reflected He who creates man to His own image. This Christian virtue is composed especially of evangelical attitudes of humility, compunction, renunciation of self, and charity above all. Here we must underline that, right from the first book, the author insists upon love: "The performance of an action is worthless in itself, if it is not done out of love" (I, 15, 1). Obedience, therefore, is not to be practised because it is necessary or useful, but through charity, for the love of God—and it is only thus that liberty of spirit grows and is preserved (I, 9, 1). Beside these fundamental virtues, others, which result from these, make their appearance: joy, simplicity, purity, truthfulness, patience, meekness.

One who approaches without prejudice the reading of the first book of the *Imitation* will find there, we think, nothing oppressive or narrow, nothing legalistic or artificial, but rather the logical development of a choice: an interior movement in the steps of Christ, with only those exigencies which this in-

terior development carries with it. This choice itself is in direct
relationship with the Sermon on the Mount concerning the intention of the heart, as well as the primacy of the spirit which
quickens over the letter which kills.

2. The Second Book

The Second Book is subtitled "Considerations Inviting Us
to Live an Interior Life." This book moves beyond the first,
through the unity of its subjects, and through its progression
towards the summit of divine friendship. "Learn to despise this
world of outward things, and devote yourself to what lies within; there, within you, you will see the coming of God's kingdom. That is what 'God's kingdom' means—peacefulness and
rejoicing in the Holy Spirit" (II, 1, 1). More intimately than
in the first book, the spiritual man is brought into contact with
Christ; indeed, when he has freed his spirit from all that occupied it unduly, he is asked to put himself aside. "Christ is
ready to come to you, with what kindness in His glance! But
you must make room, deep in your heart, to entertain Him as
He deserves" (II, 1, 1).

a) *Union with Christ* and with God through Christ is
more strongly marked: "If you love Jesus, if you love the
truth, if you really direct your gaze inwards, and rid yourself
of uncontrolled affections, then you can turn to God at will,
lifted out of yourself by an impulse of the spirit, and rest in
Him contentedly" (II, 1, 6). The grace of Jesus Christ, says
the author, here influenced by the Bernardine spirit, is accorded
the interior man: "He is a frequent visitor; such pleasant
converse, such welcome words of comfort, such deep repose,
such intimate friendship, are well-nigh past belief" (II, 1, 1).
This grace of Christ encourages the interior man to support
contradictions and humiliations. Veiled allusions, made clearer
in the third book, permit us to glimpse a heart sensitive in the
extreme, a prey to exterior contradictions, broken under interior stresses in a prayer without consolation. He has only
one recourse: Jesus, the faithful friend, with whom he finds
peace in the acceptance of suffering, and sufficient patience to
arrive at the love of the cross. In the second book we already
find affirmed a *pur amour* which penetrates into the soul and

absorbs it so that it reaches a point of no longer being occupied with what pleases or displeases it, but ignores outrages because "the love of Jesus fills us with self-contempt" (II, 1, 6).

b) It is through self-abnegation, through the example of Jesus Christ, that man arrives at *Christian wisdom.* "The man who can experience all the values of life, not judging them by what is said about them, or the price that is put upon them, but as they really are—he is the true expert; his learning is not human but divine" (II, 1, 7), that is to say, according to the only true order, that of the redemption, of Love. Aside from sin, which it destroys or rejects, the Christian order refuses nothing, but accepts all things, because in all things and according to what they are—including traces of sin and corruption— the glory of God can be manifested.

This wisdom expresses itself in those humble and specifically Christian virtues, unknown to merely natural wisdom, and which clearly characterize Christian perfection as opposed to doctrines of non-Christian perfection: humility, patience, a simple view of God in all things. The *Imitation* extols the exterior behavior of the Christian in his dealings with others: the wise person makes every effort to dwell in peace not only with gentile and benevolent people, but also with those who "are difficult and cross-grained," and who "get out of hand and keep on contradicting us" (II, 3, 2). He is not easily scandalized, but puts the best possible interpretation on everything. "You would see everything with clear eyes, fit everything into the pattern of your thought, if goodness and purity were at the roots of your being" (II, 4, 2). But the Christian must first of all *be* wise and good himself before judging outwardly any person or any matter whatsoever, for "it is what he is in himself that determines a man's judgment of what lies outside himself" (II, 4, 2). He is a man who does not justify his actions first of all by laws, the Rule, customs, or any other external reference, but rather he places himself before God *in his own conscience.*

It is certainly not the least of the merits of the second book that it takes up so boldly the defense of the enlightened and all-embracing good conscience (II, 6). The author of the *Imitation* probably experienced at his own cost how the spiritual life becomes a caricature if the conscience is oppressed, whether interiorly or exteriorly, and that formalism, false devotion, and narrowness of spirit close up and pervert the life of the soul.

c) The wise Christian, finally, is one who has acquired that *interior liberty* which leaves to God all personal glory, and leans solely upon the grace of Him who, he knows, incessantly renews his spirit (II, 8).

This liberty is acquired only by means of a complete detachment, not only from sin or from the desire for sin, but even from all consolation, whether human or divine (II, chs. 7—10). It befits the liberated soul to be grateful not only when God gives his consolation but also when He takes it away, not to keep it for himself, but to turn it back towards God in a pure state, to detach himself from it without constraint and without vainglory, judging rightly that "when he has done everything that he knows he ought to do, he should realize that he has done nothing" (II, 11, 4).

"There is never a man with greater freedom than he who knows how to renounce himself and all besides, setting himself in the lowest place of all" (II, 11, 5). Christian liberty is acquired only upon the cross of Christ. The last chapters of the second book are entirely consecrated to incorporation into Christ crucified (II, chs. 10—12). It is only on the cross that this annihilation of the natural self can take place. The more interior a man becomes, the greater also becomes his spiritual liberty, and "the weightier will he often find his crosses becoming" (II, 12, 7). Conversely, it is crosses which will help to enlarge his interior liberty. For, "the more the flesh is weakened by suffering the more is the spirit strengthened by means of inward grace" (II, 12, 8). This interior action, this action of God in the soul, is realized only by grace (II, 12, 8). Now, it is precisely the love of Jesus which calls down upon us this grace and increases it.

d) The love of Jesus causes certain persons—the author had probably known some of these—no longer to be able to bear being without pain or tribulation. If they had the choice, they would wish to suffer adversity for Christ rather than to be comforted by Him, pressed as they are by the "senseless" desire to be more like unto Him (II, 12, 8 and 14). It is indeed by the light of this love for Christ that the *Imitation* comes to teach, regarding the life which leads to the interior kingdom and the life which one leads therein: "Make no mistake about it; the life you are to lead must be one of death-in-life. The more a man dies to himself, the more he begins to live to God" (II, 12, 14).

3. The Third Book

The themes treated in the Third Book are scarcely different from those of the first two, except that love and grace are spoken of more expressly. What is striking, however, is that these themes are given quite a different type of exposition, and treated with a more profound and more affective tonality, using a variety of tones which the first two books do not present. Further, the epigrammatic monologue gives place to a dialogue between Christ and the faithful soul, the peaceful meditation to active instruction, the calm reflection to lived experience.

a) The more we familiarize ourselves with the third book, the stronger becomes our impression that we are reaching a more interior level of the *spiritual life of the author*. The chapters which follow one another apparently without much order draw the portrait of a man of astonishing spiritual vitality, who experiences in his body and in his soul all the tragedy—perhaps it would be more fitting to say all the epic character—of the ascent towards God, from the painful breaking of the ties of sin to the delights of the divine union, to the fullness of abandonment. He is a man who with all his force tends towards God, desires to be admitted to contemplate His face, and makes his own the sorrowful aspirations of so many mystics: "When will it come, that blissful and longed-for hour, when the joy of your presence shall brim to overflowing the depths of my desire, and you be my all in all?" (III, 34, 3). This man knows, through having experienced it, the sweetness of contemplation, and even jubilation and "ecstasies of joy" (III, 34, 3).

Elsewhere, he seems to have remained so earthly that he feels weighed down, "with the spirit trying to soar aloft, and the body endeavoring to stay below" (III, 48, 4). On the one hand, he expands in an atmosphere of peace and contemplation, but on the other, the trials undergone by his self-love and his extreme sensibility overwhelm him. The closer he approaches to pure love, the more pressing and more penetrating become the exigencies of humility, of abnegation, of the struggle against himself. The master of the interior life reaches in to the very roots (III, 37), and would purify the soul by warning it of the secret betrayals of nature, which seeks itself so cleverly under subtle appearances.

With a disconcerting virility, man seconds the purifying operations of grace. Painfully surprised by the tenacious roots of self-love or ill-regulated affections, of desire for praise or admiration, he exhorts himself: "Direct the fire of your anger against yourself; do not let pride, that monstrous growth, draw nourishment from you any more; but show yourself so submissive, so unimportant, that everyone may walk over you, trample you like mud in the streets" (III, 13, 3).

This man aspires towards God, but through experience he knows what it is to be distracted from God by a world of sensations, pleasures, and erroneous doctrines. Where is he to find support? In human knowledge? He has experienced its limits (III, 31, 2). In prayer? But without the consolation of grace, this prayer is troubled by unrest and distraction, by the temptations of the flesh (III, 49, 2; 48, 24), tormented by evil tongues which would destroy his good reputation. How can he hope to establish his peace in men (III, chs. 28—31)?

However, that part of him which is already submissive to wisdom does not permit itself to be overthrown by the judgment of men (III, 28, 1). For in his wisdom he does not desire to please men, but neither does he fear to displease them (III, 28, 2). He knows how to avoid those who flatter him, and to bear prudently with those who contradict him (III, 27, 5). He loves virtue and simplicity; he hates all false speech. He asks of God to put true words upon his lips, and to fend off all error from his conduct. Above all, he is humble, and is not saddened by the fact that he enjoys little renown (III, 22, 4), and finds his joy and peace in doing the will of others. He prefers to have little rather than much, and seeks the last place (III, 23, 3). His heart and his spirit are already raised so high as to cause him to suffer from seeing so little seriousness and spirituality among his fellows, and from the fact that they remain so outwardly distracted and, as it were, prisoners of the outward appearance of things (III, 44, 2).

Although he has vowed his life to union with God, he knows himself henceforth well enough to realize that he is not ripe for contemplation (III, 4, 4) and that he must still pass through many purifying trials.

Of what sort are these interior trials? A passage from chapter 49 gives some idea of them: "Often you will have to do what you dislike, and forego doing what you would like to do. Other people's interests will prosper, your own will make no headway; others will be listened to when they speak, but people will take no notice of anything you say. Others will ask for things, and get them; when you ask, your request will be in vain" (III, 49, 4).

b) But the *real heart of the trial* lies elsewhere: not only does he feel himself betrayed by his own nature, beaten down by trials, rejected by men, but, what is more, he is bound to condemn his own conscience, and he can no longer find in it any support or build a foundation upon it. In fact, contrary to the first book, where the author placed all his confidence in a pure heart, here he no longer dares to find justification in his conscience; henceforth he can hope only in God. "O Lord my God, you are my total good; who am I to dare to speak to you?" (III, 3, 6). In this way, he reaches the point of taking God's part against himself (III, 52, 3); it is good that God has not spared his faults, but has afflicted him with anguish, sending him distress, both within and without (III, 50, 5). He considers himself of less worth than anyone else, and, if he sees others commit sin, he can say to himself in all truth: "You ought to have a poorer opinion of yourself than of them, and deem no one to be weaker than yourself" (III, 28, 1).

c) Grace and love. Still, he neither gives up the fight nor loses himself in sorrowful complaints, but he seeks refuge and strength in prayer (II, 50, 5). It is through God, in God, and for God that this man bears with his rebellious nature, his past marked by sin, his numerous trials, and his own powerlessness to find God (III, 35), and not through his own strength. If he has ventured upon the search for God, if he continues it, it is because, drawn by grace, he advances into the merciful heart of God. A constant appeal to grace makes itself heard throughout the whole of the third book (III, 19, 5; 23, 9; 31, 1; 55): "Yes, I need your grace, and a lot of it at that, if I am to overcome nature" (III, 55, 2 and 4). To lose oneself in grace belongs to love alone. Love requires that man, in a depth of imperturbable peace, allow himself to be detached not only from every external desire—a detachment which brings him interior peace—but even from all interior support, which will lead him to union with God. Love demands the gift of all things (III, 55, 4); of creatures, of oneself, even of God for God's sake.

It is here that the author attains to the summit of the imitation of Christ, and that he gains a place among the most authentic Christian mystics. We cannot doubt that the heroic abnegation of himself has been accompanied by signal graces.

Without having positively sought them—our author really aims above all at interior peace and liberty, stability in faith, confidence, and love of God—he has undoubtedly been favored with these graces. From time to time, he would have known those *excessus mentis,* which elevate the soul above its earthly condition and transport it into God. More habitually, however, he would have been favored by an interior light, "a savor, a movement, an austere and sweet force which springs from the depth of the soul, where God dwells . . . Caring less for introspection than for useful truth, he does not think of recounting his mystical ascensions, but rather of repeating to himself what it was good for him to hear and to answer."[5]

All these graces he has won in the midst of a great struggle, and this struggle has increased his stature. The third book of the *Imitation* shows us a man who, surmounting his own trials, cares about offering to his brothers the fruits of his experience. This experience informs a teaching full of profound truth on the spiritual life. We find, in fact, few such heights of teaching in all of Christian literature. We have but to reread the chapters on compunction (III, 52), on the happiness of wisdom in God (ch. 34), on the grandeurs of grace (chs. 53—55), on the discernment of spirits (chs. 50—52), on the diversity of the movements of nature and of grace (ch. 54)—the jewel of the entire book!—on the jubilations of love: "The divine charity overcomes everything, gives every power of the soul room to expand" (ch. 9, 12).

This accomplished practitioner of Christian asceticism becomes a great expert in divine love. He experiences love not only in ecstatic transports; he has also found that it penetrates and purifies the deepest layers of his psychological life, triumphing over every inferiority complex, annihilating every tendency to narcissism, liberating from neurosis: "If heavenly grace gains entrance to your heart, together with real charity, there will be no envy there, no shriveling of the heart, no monopolizing of your affections by any particular love" (III, 9, 11).

d) Divine love gives clairvoyance in *discernment of spirits.* Not every interior desire, attests the author, comes from the Holy Spirit, and it is often difficult to discern by what spirit one is moved. With a rare perspicacity, the *Imitation* discourses at length on the dangers of *indiscreet devotion;* this subject, already broached in the first book, is here treated more fully. Instructed by his own experience, and undoubtedly also by his companions and by books, the author knows what snares are laid for union with God by a disorderly attachment to sensible consolations. He must have been acquainted with some of those imprudent persons who, not having known how to put *devotion* below humility, preferring to follow the desires of their heart rather than the judgment of right reason, or again refusing the counsels of an experienced director, go astray and run into shipwreck (III, 7, 8, and 10). Without, for all that, rejecting spiritual consolations, the author adopts in their regard a supple attitude, holding solidly to two points of view: that grace which attracts to abnegation and to the purity of love is not opposed to affectionate outbursts of the heart; on the contrary, it often gives rise to them, at least in certain stages of the spiritual life. On the other hand, the number and the perfection of the divine visits are not the norm of Christian perfection.

"A man is not to be accounted as full of merit for often seeing visions or feeling divine consolation, or being a great Biblical scholar or being raised to a higher dignity. No, a man is

meritorious when his spiritual life is based on real humility,
when he is full of the love of God; he is always seeking, purely
and wholly, the honor of God; when he thinks of himself as
good for nothing, really takes a poor view of himself" (III, 7,
2). The golden rule in this matter is the following: "The more
you can leave yourself behind, my son, the more you will be
able to enter into me" (III, 56, 1).

4. The Fourth Book

Although the Fourth Book is clearly distinguished from the
first three, both by subject and by arrangement, this final little
work may nevertheless be regarded as the summit of the whole
of the *Imitation*. Here, in fact, the fervent Christian discovers
the meaning of his ardent desires for the Eucharistic presence:
"In order that I may be but one spirit with Thee" (IV, 14).
What was sought after in the first three books and never fully
found, union with God, is here attained in the heart of the
Eucharistic mystery—if not in the clarity of the vision and
the plenitude of possession, at least in the surrender of faith.

The fourth book is entirely consecrated to the praise, the
explanation, and the penetration of the Eucharistic mystery.
It is, with the hymns of Saint Thomas Aquinas, the finest text
of the second half of the Middle Ages on Eucharistic devotion
and mysticism. Affectivity is everywhere here present, over-
shadowing somewhat the care for intellectual penetration. Love,
which is also a form of knowledge, perceives more clearly, because it is better attuned to it, the central sacrament of the faith.

"It is not frivolity that draws us here, not curiosity, not a desire for sensual pleasure, but firm faith, devout hope, and love
unfeigned" (IV, 1, 9). With an ardor more sustained than in
the preceding books, the author entertains his desire and nourishes his piety in view of the Mass to be celebrated, the Communion to be received. He penetrates its excellence, its awe-
some grandeur, but also its true sweetness and necessity. In
his analysis of the fourth book, Père Debongnie shows us the
author as a "person buffeted between confusion and desire,
and who progressively, without ever neglecting to humiliate
himself, makes bold with confidence and love to draw near."[6]
Two truths are made evident, to which correspond two duties
to be fulfilled: on the one hand, the divine excellence of the

Eucharist and the essential unworthiness of man; on the other,
the call of Christ to man to unite himself to Him, and the desire which He enkindles in the docile heart: "In so dealing with
your chosen you have a purpose. It is to make them conscious
of the truth, by their own plain experience, that by themselves
they are extremely weak, and that from you they gain an immense store of goodness and grace" (IV, 4, 3). Hence the
necessity of a profound humility and purity of conscience.

The fourth book, one might say, carries the imitation of
Christ by his faithful follower to its final consequence: the
completely pure glorification of God. It allows us to perceive
that the "success" of the Christian life consists finally not in
the accomplishment of a love which, seconded by grace, man
seeks and pursues by means of his own lights and resources,
but rather in the welcome, the acceptance, by man of a Love
which gives Itself through Itself (IV, 12, 3). In the mystery
of the Eucharistic union, all glory rests with Love Itself. When
man no longer seeks anything for himself, but has in view only
the glory and the good pleasure of God, only then begins in
earnest the *interior life* properly so called: that of God, Who
glorifies Himself in man. It is towards this glory that the
fourth book aspires: "When he receives the Holy Eucharist,
he merits the great grace of union with God, for he is not
concerned with his own devotion or comfort. Beyond all devotion and consolation, this is what he seeks: the honor and
glory of God" (IV, 15, 4).

Conclusion

Our presentation of the *Imitation of Christ* has been directed
to the book in itself, such as it is presented to the reader, in-
dependently of the problematical aspects which in our day
have grown up around it. It has been offered to us as a book
which, having opted for the way of interiorization of the Christian life, is written with a view to practice and experience;
and these are conceived as a progressive ascent towards union
with God.

The author of the *Imitation* is among those who esteem that
a deep sense of life is found only in interiority. Let us agree,
this point of view is restricted, denoting an individualistic, subjective mentality; it ill satisfies the objective demands and the

desire for action of the modern mentality. People have applied
themselves to show that the author of the *Imitation* neglects to
consider an objective understanding of the mysteries of the
faith and of the sacramental life, and that he flees the exterior
world, or at least avoids human society. It has been pointed
out that the work lacks a theology of the Church, a liturgical
spirit in the precise sense of this expression, a Biblical theology
also, for the Holy Scripture is not first of all a book of spiritual
and moral maxims. Finally, it is reproached with underlining
almost exclusively the vertical dimension of Christianity, and
of being uninterested in its horizontal dimensions. These judg-
ments doubtless contain their part of truth.

However, if we wish to render justice to the author of the
Imitation, let us not blame him for having kept within the
limits of the very nature of his work. It is precisely from respect for these limits that the *Imitation* receives its strength
and the extraordinary unity of its form, which place it among
the masterpieces of spiritual literature. If certain dimensions
of the Christian life, to which the modern mentality is particularly sensitive, have not held the attention of the author, it is
primarily because, as a man of his time, he shared the ensemble
of the values and habits of mind of his epoch; after which let
us remark that without including *expressis verbis* those dimensions which today are so important, he did not exclude them
either; finally, their absence does not cause the work to miss
its aim, which is to lead the soul by way of contemplation and
imitation of Christ to union with God. The author of the
Imitation did not set out to include *everything* that may lead
a man to an authentic spiritual life. He simply said what, in
his eyes, formed the essence of this life, and what, again in
his own eyes, constituted *an excellent way* for attaining thereto.
Then, even if he were writing in our days, it seems to us that,
without in any way renouncing modern approaches, he could
still retain all the vigor of two essential principles of the Christian life, which are at the basis of his work: on the one hand,
the primacy of contemplation over action, and that of love of
God over love of neighbor;[7] and on the other hand, the Gospel
maxim, "If any man would come after me, let him deny himself and take up his cross and follow me" (Mt 16:24).

Notes*

NOTES TO CHAPTER 1

[1] Augustine, *Holy Virginity* 27, FC 27, 174.

[2] J. Guitton, *The Problem of Jesus* (New York, 1955) 111.

[3] See J. de Fraine, *Adam and the Family of Man* (New York 1965).

[4] See P. Gutierrez, *La paternité spirituelle selon saint Paul*, Études bibliques (Paris, 1968) 33, nn. 2 and 3.

[5] See also 1 Mc 2:51-64, and the *Testaments of the Twelve Patriarchs*, an apocryphal writing dating undoubtedly back to the first century before Jesus Christ.

[6] Epictetus, *Discourses* 2.14.12-13, Loeb Classical Library (Cambridge, Mass., 1956) 308-309; see DS, vol. 4, cols. 825-827.

[7] See art. "Église grecque," DS, vol. 6, cols. 814-815.

[8] See art. "Conversion," DS, vol. 2, cols. 2232-2235.

[9] J. Ratzinger, *Introduction to Christianity* (New York, 1970) 157-159.

[10] See R. Schnackenburg, *The Moral Teaching of the New Testament* (Freiburg 1965) 161-163.

[11] See E. J. Tinsley, *The Imitation of God in Christ. An Essay on the Basis of Christian Spirituality* (London, 1960).

[12] M. Dibelius, *From Tradition to Gospel* (New York, no date) 37-69.

[13] E. Lohmeyer, *Das Evangelium des Markus*, 1st ed. (Gottingen, 1937) 31-33.

[14] A. Schulz, *Suivre et imiter le Christ...* (Paris, 1966) 16.

---

* Since this series is intended for English readers only, many of the references in the original articles of the DS to publications in foreign languages have been omitted. All titles of primary sources have been translated into their English equivalents. Where quotations from foreign works are given in the body of the text, reference is made in the footnotes to the book or article from which the translation has been taken or made.

[15] B. Gerhardsson, *Memory and Manuscript. Oral Tradition and Written Transmission in Rabbinic Judaism and Early Christianity* (Upsala, 1961).

[16] K. H. Rengstorf, *"Manthanō,"* in TDNT, vol. 4, 391-413.

[17] M. Hengel, *Nachfolge und Charisma . . .* (Berlin, 1968).

[18] "To follow after" appears in anecdotes referring to a journey, according to M. Hengel, op. cit., 57, and ordinarily does not have the meaning of "to be a disciple of." See also ibid., 56.

[19] A. Schulz, *op. cit.,* 55 and 37.

[20] Examples in B. Gerhardsson, *op. cit.,* 181-189.

[21] See W. D. Davis, *The Setting of the Sermon on the Mount* (Cambridge, 1964) 455-457.

[22] See art. "Conseils évangeliques," DS, vol. 2, cols. 1592-1609.

[23] E. Dinkler, "Jesu Wort vom Kreuztragen," *Neutestamentliche Studien für R. Bultmann* (Berlin, 1954) 110-129.

[24] J. Jeremias, *"Pais theou,"* in TDNT, vol. 5, 677-717.

[25] M. Hengel, *Die Zeloten* (Leiden and Cologne, 1961) 266.

[26] J. Gwyn Griffiths, "The Disciple's Cross," *New Testament Studies* 16 (1970) 358-364.

[27] N. A. Dahl, "Formgeschichtliche Beobachtungen zur Christusverkündigung in der Gemeindepredigt," in *Neutestamentliche Studien für R. Bultmann* (Berlin, 1954) 3-9.

[28] Th. Aerts, "Suivre Jésus. Évolution d'un thème biblique dans les évangiles synoptiques," *Ephemerides theologicae lovanienses* 42 (1966) 492.

[29] See art. "Eucharistie," DS, vol. 4, cols. 1553-1565.

[30] Mk. 10:38 adds "and to be baptized with the baptism with which I am to be baptized?"; see A. Feuillet, "La coupe et le baptême de la Passion," *Revue biblique* 74 (1967) 356-391.

[31] A. Feuillet, *op. cit.,* 363.

[32] *Ibid.,* 376.

[33] *Ibid.,* 383-384.

[34] Th. Aerts, *op. cit.,* 484-485.

[35] É. Trocmé, " 'Avec Jésus' et 'en Christ'," *Revue d'histoire et de philosophie religieuses* 42 (1962) 228.

[36] I Thes 1:6; 2 Thes 3:7 and 9; 1 Cor 4:16 and 11:1.

[37] See J. Goetz et al., *A Christian Anthropology* in the present series.

[38] See art. "Image et ressemblance," DS, vol. 7, cols. 1404-1405.

[39] Besides the commentaries, see C. M. Proudfoot, "Imitation or Realistic Participation? A Study of Paul's Concept of 'Suffering with Christ'," *Interpretation* 17 (1963) 140-160.

[40] L. Cerfaux, *The Christian in the Theology of St. Paul* (New York, 1967) 88.

[41] David Stanley, "Paul and the Christian Concept of the Servant of God," in *The Apostolic Church in the New Testament* (Westminster, Md., 1965) 312-351.

[42] See R. P. Martin, *Phil 2:5-11 in Recent Interpretation and in in the Setting of Early Christian Worship* (Cambridge, 1967).

[43] See C. H. Dodd, *"Ennomos Christou,"* in *Studia Paulina in honorem J. de Zwaan* (Haarlem, 1953) 96-110; W. D. Davies, *The Setting of the Sermon on the Mount* (Cambridge, 1964) 341-366.

[44] E. Larsson, *Christus als Vorbild* (Upsala, 1962) 74-80.

[45] A. Plummer, *The Second Epistle of St. Paul to the Corinthians*, International Critical Commentary (New York, 1915) 273.

[46] See below, chapter 2.

[47] David Stanley, " 'Become Imitators of Me': the Pauline Conception of Apostolic Tradition," *Biblica* 40 (1959) 859-877.

[48] W. P. de Boer, *The Imitation of Paul* (Kampen, 1962).

[49] David Stanley, *op. cit.*, 865.

[50] Oscar Cullmann, *The Christology of the New Testament* (Philadelphia, 1959) 74.

[51] See R. H. Gundry, " 'Verba Christi' in 1 Peter: Their Implications Concerning the Authorship of 1 Peter and the Authenticity of the Gospel Tradition," *New Testament Studies* 13 (1967) 336-350.

[52] R. Thysman, "L'éthique de l'imitation du Christ dans le nouveau Testament. Situation, notations et variations du thème," *Ephemerides theologicae lovanienses* 42 (1966) 138-175.

[53] A. Schulz, *op. cit.*, (note 14), 108.

[54] See art. "Jean (saint)," DS, vol. 7, cols. 214-216; 235-237.

[55] *Pisteuein eis* (3:18.36, etc.). See art. "Foi," DS, vol. 5. col. 541.

[56] See A. Schulz, *op. cit.*, (note 14), 70.

[57] This is contrary to Schulz, *ibid.*, 81, who sees it simply as an accompaniment.

[58] *Mekhilta* on Ex 14:15, quoted by M. Hengel, op. cit. (note 17), 24-25.

[59] Jn 15:14-15; see C. Spicq, *Agape in the New Testament*, vol. 3 (St. Louis, 1966) 43-48.

[60] N. Lazure, *Les valeurs morales de la théologie johannique*, Études bibliques (Paris, 1965) 56-47.

[61] For a comparison with the Synoptic *logia*, see C. H. Dodd, *Historical Tradition in the Fourth Gospel* (Cambridge, 1963) 338-343.

[62] A. Weers, *Contribution à une recherche sur l'idée d'imitation dans les écrits johanniques*, Faculty of Theology of Lyons, mimeographed thesis (Lyons, 1966-1967).

[63] N. Lazure, *op. cit.*, 59.

[64] J.-M.-R. Tillard, "L'Eucharistie et la fraternité," *Nouvelle revue théologique* 91 (1969) 133.

[65] J. Rademakers, "Mission et apostolat dan l'Évangile johannique," in *Studia evangelica*, Texte und Untersuchungen 87 (Berlin, 1964) 119.

[66] On the meaning of "new", see C. Spicq, *Agape in the New Testament*, vol. 3 (St. Louis, 1966) 53.

[67] C. H. Dodd, "A Hidden Parable in the 4th Gospel," in *More New Testament Studies* (Grand Rapids, 1968) 30-40.

[68] E.g. 1 Jn 1:6-7; 2:6; 3:7; 3 Jn 7.

[69] A. Weers, *op. cit.*, 155.

[70] J. Rademakers, *op. cit.*, (note 65) 121.

NOTES TO CHAPTER 2

[1] See art. "État," DS, vol. 4, cols. 1372-1388.

[2] See art. "Ascèse," DS, vol. 1, cols. 964-977, in which these forms are seen in relation to asceticism.

[3] See L. Bouyer, *The Spirituality of the New Testament and the Fathers* (New York, 1963) 190-210, 303-330.

[4] See art. "Étienne (saint)," DS, vol. 4, cols. 1477-1481.

[5] Acts 7:56 refers back to Lk 22:69: "But from now on the Son of man shall be seated at the right hand of the power of God."

[6] X. Leon-Dufour, "Les Évangiles et l'histoire de Jésus," *Études* 316 (1963) 158.

[7] See arts. "Ennemis (Amour des)," "Étienne (saint)," DS, vol. 4, cols. 761, 1480-1481.

[8] Saint Cyprian, *Book on the Value of Patience* in *Treatises*, FC 36, 279.

[9] *Sacramentarium veronense*, ed. L. C. Mohlberg (Rome, 1956) 86, 88.

[10] See art. "Ignace d'Antioche (saint)," DS, vol. 7, cols. 1250-1266.

[11] Ignatius of Antioch, Rom. 3:5-6 in *The Epistles of St. Clement of Rome and St. Ignatius of Antioch*, ACW 1, 81-83.

[12] Th. Preiss, "La mystique de l'imitation du Christ et de l'unité chez Ignace...," *Revue d'histoire et de philosophie religieuses* 18 (1938) 212, about H. von Campenhausen, *Die Idee des Martyriums* (Göttingen, 1936) 73.

[13] Ignatius of Antioch, Smyrn. 4 in *The Epistles...*, ACW 1. 91.

[14] Ignatius of Antioch, Smyrn. 4 in *The Epistles...*, ACW 1. 91. 87-88: see Polycarp, Phil. 8 and 10 in *The Didache...The Epistles and the Martyrdom of St. Polycarp*, ACW 6, 79-80.

[15] Ignatius of Antioch, Rom. 7 in *The Epistles...*, ACW 1, 83.

NOTES   111

16 *Martyrdom of St. Polycarp* 1 and 10 in *The Didache* ..., ACW 6, 90-99.

17 Eusebius, *Ecclesiastical History*, FC 29, 288.

18 Eusebius, *Ecclesiastical History*, FC 19, 417; see the case of Blandina, *ibid.*, 424-432.

19 Origen, *Exhortation to Martyrdom*, ACW 19, 141-196.

20 Cyprian, *Exhortation to Martyrdom, to Fortunatus*, FC 36, 311-344.

21 Cyprian, *ibid.*, 5, FC 36, 323.

22 Origen, *Exhortation to Martyrdom* 12, ACW 19, 152-153.

23 Origen, *ibid.*, 13, ACW 19, 153-154.

24 Origen, *ibid.*, 36, ACW 19, 179.

25 Origen, *ibid.*

26 Origen, *ibid.*, 32, 37; see 30, ACW 19, 172, 181; see 171.

27 Origen, *ibid.*, 28, 40, ACW 19, 168, 184.

28 Origen, *ibid.*, 41, citing 1 Jn 3:16, ACW 19, 185.

29 Origen, *ibid.*, 41-44, ACW 19, 184-187.

30 Origen, *ibid.*, 37, ACW 19, 180.

31 See E. L. Hummel, *The Concept of Martyrdom according to St. Cyprian* (Washington, 1946); art. "Conversion," DS, vol. 2 cols. 2261-2269.

32 Leo the Great, *Sermon* 85.1, NPNF, 2nd ser. vol. 12, 197.

33 Irenaeus, *Against Heresies* 3.12.13 in ANF, vol. 1, 435.

34 See various dictionaries sub verbo. See also E. J. Tinsley, "The *Imitatio Christi* in the Mysticism of St. Ignatius ...," *Studia patristica*, Texte und Untersuchungen 2 (Berlin, 1955) 553-560; L. Bouyer, *The Spirituality of the New Testament and the Fathers* (New York, 1963) 199-201.

35 É. Mersch, *The Whole Christ* (Milwaukee, 1938) 330.

36 John Chrysostom, *Homilies on St. John's Gospel* 49.1, FC 41, 12.

37 John Chrysostom, *Against the Anomoeans* 10.2.

38 John Chrysostom, *The Joys of the Future Life* 5.

39 John Chrysostom, *On "Father, if it is possible, let it pass"* 4.

40 John Chrysostom, *Against the Jews* 8.9.

41 John Chrysostom, *Homilies on Philippians* 6.1, NPNF, 1st ser., vol. 13, 206.

42 John Chrysostom, *Homilies on Romans* 24.4, NPNF, 1st ser., vol. 11, 520-521.

43 John Chrysostom, *Homilies on the Acts* 14.4, ibid., 92.

44 John Chrysostom, *Homilies on the Gospel of St. Matthew*, 78.4, NPNF, 1st ser., vol. 10, 473.

45 John Chrysostom, *Homilies on St. John's Gospel* 15.3, FC 33, 148.

46 John Chrysostom, *Homilies on Philippians* 13.1, NPNF, 1st

112 NOTES

[47] John Chrysostom, *Against Those Who Lodge Virgins in Their Communities* 3.

[48] John Chrysostom, *Homilies on St. John's Gospel* 31.3, FC 33, 130.

[49] John Chrysostom, *Homilies on the Gospel of St. Matthew* 30.5, NPNF, 1st ser., vol. 10, 202.

[50] L. Bouyer, *The Spirituality of the New Testament and the Fathers* (New York, 1963) 443-444.

[51] John Chrysostom, *Homilies on 1 Corinthians* 8.7, NPNF, 1st ser., vol. 12, 47.

[52] E. Mersch, *op. cit.*, (note 35), 324-325.

[53] John Chrysostom, *Homilies on 1 Corinthians* 42.1, NPNF, 1st ser., 12; see L. J. Ohleyer, *The Pauline Formula "induere Christum" with Special Reference to the Works of St. John Chrysostom* (Washington, 1921) 254.

[54] John Chrysostom, *Commentary on Galatians* 3.5, NPNF, 1st ser., vol. 13, 30.

[55] John Chrysostom, *Homilies on Ephesians* 3.2-4, ibid., 62-63.

[56] John Chrysostom, *Homilies on St. John's Gospel* 19.3, FC 33, 191.

[57] John Chrysostom, *Homilies on Romans* 15.6, NPNF, 1st ser., vol. 11, 457-458.

[58] John Chrysostom, *Baptismal Instructions*, 1.29,31 ACW 31, 34-35.

[59] L. Meyer, *Saint Jean Chrysostome, maitre de perfection chretienne* (Paris, 1934) 219.

[60] See art. "Augustine (saint)," DS, vol. 1, cols. 1110-1111.

[61] 1) Christ the way and true path of the Christian: *Sermon* 141.4; 2) *The Christian Combat* 11 (12), and 33 (35), in *Writings of St. Augustine: Christian Instruction. Admonition and Grace. The Christian Combat. Faith, Hope and Charity.* FC 2, 327-330, 352-353; 3) Christ as Wisdom in *The Trinity* 7.3.5, FC 45, 226-227; 4) The humble Christ: see art. "Humilité," DS, vol. 7, cols. 1153-1154.

[62] See art. "Ascèse," DS, vol. 1, col. 978; see also I. Noye et al., *Jesus in Christian Devotion and Contemplation* in the present series.

[63] Bernard, *Concerning Grace and Free Will* 10 (New York, 1920) 52-57.

[64] Bernard, *The Steps of Humility* 1.1; 7.21 (Cambridge, Mass., 1950) 122-123, 162-163.

[65] Bernard, *On the Love of God* 3-4 (Trappist, Kentucky, 1943) 11-19.

[66] Bernard, *On the Song of Songs* 20.6, CF 4, 152.

[67] Bernard, *On the Song of Songs* 43.4 (Dublin, 1920) vol. 1, 496.

[68] Bernard, *On the Song of Songs* 20.8, CF 4, 154.

[69] Bernard, *Sermon for Spy Wednesday* 12 in *St. Bernard's Sermons for the Seasons and Principal Festivals of the Year* (Westminster, Md., 1960) vol. 2, 150.

[70] Bernard, *The Steps of Humility* 1.1; 4.15 (Cambridge, Mass., 1950) 122-123, 148, 151.

[71] A. Van Den Bosch, excerpts of a doctoral thesis in *Collectanea ordinis cisterciensium reformatorum* 21-23 (1959-1961), in particular "Le Christ, Dieu devenu imitable d'après S. Bernard," 22 (1960) 341-355.

[72] See Bernard, *Sermon for Advent* 4.4, op. cit. (note 69) vol. 1, 44-45.

[73] Bernard, *Sermon for the Nativity* 1.2, ibid., vol. 1, 383-384.

[74] Bernard, *Sermon for Spy Wednesday* 11, ibid., vol. 2,14 9.

[75] Bernard, *Concerning Grace and Free Will* 10 (New York, 1920) 53.

[76] *Ibid.*, 55-56.

[77] *Ibid.*, 56. See art. "Dissemblance" (in St. Bernard), DS, vol. 3, cols. 1338-1342. See also art, "Bernard," DS vol. 1, esp. cols. 1481-1485; "Humilitè," ibid., cols. 1164-1166 and in this series, I. Noye et al., *Jesus in Christian Contemplation and Devotion*, RES 1.

[78] Francis of Assisi, *Counsels* 21 in *St. Francis of Assisi* (New York, 1959) 176.

[79] See art. "François d'Assise (saint)," DS, vol. 5, cols. 1271-1303; in book form: E. Longpré, *François d'Assise*, Bibliothèque de spiritualité 4, (Paris, 1966).

[80] Francis of Assisi, *Letters* 1.1 in *St. Francis of Assisi* (New York, 1959) 181.

[81] Francis of Assisi, *Rule* 1.22 and *Letters* 3 in *op. cit.*, 221, 191.

[82] Francis of Assisi, *Rule* 1.1, ibid., 205.

[83] Francis of Assisi, *Letters* 7 to Brother Leo, ibid., 197.

[84] Francis of Assisi, *Rule* 1.9, ibid., 212.

[85] Francis of Assisi, ibid.

[86] Francis of Assisi, *Letters* 8, ibid., 198.

[87] Francis of Assisi, *Counsels* 6, ibid., 172.

[88] Francis of Assisi, *Rule* 1.1; 2.1, ibid., 205, 228.

[89] Francis of Assisi, *Rule* 1.3; 2.3, ibid., 207-208, 228.

[90] Francis of Assisi, *Rule*, 1.9; 2.6; ibid., 212-213, 231.

[91] Francis of Assisi, *Rule* 2.9, ibid., 232-233.

[92] Francis of Assisi, *Rule* 1.16, ibid., 216-217.

[93] Francis of Assisi, *Rule* 1.22, ibid., 221.

[94] Francis of Assisi, *Rule* 1.6, *ibid.*, 210.

[95] Francis of Assisi, *Counsels* 5, *ibid.*, 171-172.

[96] Francis of Assisi, *Rule* 1.11, *ibid.*, 214.

[97] Francis of Assisi, *Counsels* 6, *ibid.*, 172.

[98] Francis of Assisi, *Testament* 14, *ibid.*, 201.

[99] Thomas de Celano, *Life* 1.9.22 in *Early Franciscan Classics* (Paterson, New Jersey, 1962) 28.

[100] Thomas de Celano, *Life* 2, pt. 1, chap. 31. Only sections of *Life* 2 are translated by N. Wydenbruck and edited by O. Karrer in *St. Francis of Assisi, The Legends and Lauds* (New York, 1948) 33-59.

[101] Thomas de Celano, *Life* 1.12.29-30; *Life* 2, pt. 2, chap. 29.

[102] Thomas de Celano, *Life* 2, pt. 2, chap. 162, *op. cit.*, 58.

[103] See art, "François d'Assise," DS, vol. 5, cols. 1298-1300.

[104] J.-H. Sbaralea, *Bullarium franciscanum*, vol. 1 (Rome, 1759) 42.

[105] *The Testament of St. Clare* in *The Legend and Writings of St. Clare of Assisi* (St. Bonaventure, New York, 1953) 85.

[106] K. Esser, *L'ordre de saint François* (Paris, 1957) 26.

[107] Thomas de Celano, *Life* 2, pt. 2, proemium.

[108] Thomas de Celano, *Life* 2, pt. 2, chap. 162, *op. cit.*, 58-59.

[109] Pius XI, *Rite expiatis, Acta Apostolicae Sedis* 18 (1926) 154.

[110] Francis of Assisi, *Rule* 1.5, in *St. Francis of Assisi* (New York, 1959) 209.

[111] Francis of Assisi, *Counsels* 1, *ibid.*, 168-169.

[112] Francis of Assisi, *Rule* 1.23, *ibid.*, 224.

[113] Francis of Assisi, *Letters* 7, *ibid.*, 197.

[114] See art. "François d'Assise (saint)," DS, cols. 1271-1302.

[115] See in particular his *Epistola de imitatione Christi* and his *Apologia pauperum*, chaps. 1-4, in *Opera*, vol. 8 (Quaracci, 1898) 499-503, 233-257.

[116] E.g., Thomas Aquinas, *Commentary on Ephesians*, chap. 5, lect. 1 (Albany, New York, 1966) 194-196; *Commentary on 1 Corinthians*, chap. 5, lect. 1.

[117] See in the present series I. Noye et al., *Jesus in Christian Contemplation and Devotion*, RES 1.

[118] See art. "Ignace de Loyola (saint), "DS, vol. 7, cols. 1289-1292; on the *Spiritual Exercises*, see *ibid.*, cols. 1315-1317.

[119] Ignatius of Loyola, *Spiritual Exercises*, nos. 95, 98, 104, 109, 147, 167-168, etc.

[120] See art. "Bremond (Henri)," DS, vol. 1, cols, 1928-1938.

[121] See art. "Bérulle," DS, vol. 1, cols. 1539-1581; "État," *ibid.*, vol.4, cols. 1378-1380; P. Pourrat, *Christian Spirituality*, vol. 3 (Westminster, Md., 1953) 356-381.

[122] Pierre de Bérulle, *Discours de l'état et des grandeurs de Jésus, par l'union inoffable do la divinité avec l'humanité, et de la dépendance et servitude qui lui est due...*, disc. 8.11, ed. Migne (Paris, 1856) col. 308.

[123] *Ibid.*, disc. 2.13, cols. 183-184.

[124] *Ibid.*, disc. 2.6, col. 168.

[125] *Ibid.*, disc. 2.11-12, col 181.

[126] *Ibid.*, disc. 2.7, col. 168.

[127] Pierre de Bérulle, *De la perpétuité des mystères de Jésus-Christ, Opuscule 77*, ed. Migne (Paris, 1856) col. 1052.

[128] See art. "Abnégation," DS, vol. 1, cols. 96-99.

[129] Pierre de Bérulle, *Mémorial de direction pour les superieurs*, chaps. 10-12, ed. Migne (Paris, 1856) cols. 817-818.

[130] Pierre de Bérulle, *Letter* 123 in *Correspondance*, ed. J. Dagens, vol. 1 (Paris, 1937) 218.

[131] G. Rotureau, introduction to the re-edition of Pierre de Bérulle, *Opuscules de piété* (Paris, 1944) 62.

[132] C. Taveau, *Le cardinal de Bérulle, maître de vie spirituelle* (Paris, 1933) 175.

[133] J. Gauthier, *L'Esprit de l'École française de spiritualité* (Paris, 1937) 104.

[134] Pierre de Bérulle, *Opuscule 29*, ed Migne (Paris, 1856) cols. 959-961.

[135] Pierre de Bérulle, *Conférences*, unedited, Municipal Library, Marseilles, ms 467, 74.

[136] Pierre de Bérulle, *Lettre 42* in *Correspondance*, ed. J. Dagens, vol. 1 (Paris, 1937) 87. See other analogous examples: *Lettres* 110, 127, 181 ibid., 195-199, 224, 317; *Opuscules* 127, 144, 186, ed. Migne (Paris, 1856) cols. 1160, 1185, 1261-1262.

[137] Pierre de Bérulle, *Discours de l'etat et des grandeurs...*, disc. 2.12-13, ed. Migne (Paris, 1856) cols. 181-182.

[138] Pierre de Bérulle, *Opuscule 198*, ed. Migne (Paris, 1856). See this text in its entirety; it treats the "three lives" of the Son of God: His glorious life, His life on earth, His interior life.

[139] H. Bremond, *Histoire...*, vol. 5; see vol. 3, 391-397. It has been noticed since then how much this judgment of Bremond needs nuancing.

[140] See DS, vol. 1, cols. 407-409.

[141] Antoine Le Gaudier, *De sanctissimi Christi Jesu Dei et hominis amore* (Pont-à-Mousson, 1619), FT (Paris, 1620); *De vera Christi Jesu...imitatione* (Paris, 1620), FT (Paris, 1630).

[142] See DS, vol. 2, cols. 2422-2423.

[143] See DS, vol. 6, cols. 53-64.

[144] See The *Spiritual Doctrine of Father Louis Lallemant* (West-

minster, Md., 1946) 108. (The present translator has given her own version from the French original.)

¹⁴⁵ *Ibid.*, 199.

¹⁴⁶ *Ibid.*, 200.

¹⁴⁷ *Ibid.*, 238.

¹⁴⁸ *Ibid.*, 240.

¹⁴⁹ *Ibid.*, 241-242.

¹⁵⁰ *Ibid.*, 245.

¹⁵¹ *Ibid.*, 246-248.

¹⁵² *Ibid.*, 248-250.

¹⁵³ *Ibid.*, 251.

¹⁵⁴ *Ibid.*, 252.

^{154a} The original article indicates here a specialized bibliography in French.

¹⁵⁵ In particular on the Sacred Heart, see art. "Coeur (Sacre)," DS, vol. 2, cols. 1023-1046.

¹⁵⁶ See the bibliography in the original article.

¹⁵⁷ M. Viller in *RAM* 27 (1951) 132-174, especially 168-172; see also "La mystique de la Passion chez S. Paul de la Croix," *Recherches de science religieuse* 40 (1952) 426-445.

¹⁵⁸ *Lettere di S. Paolo...*, vol. 1 (Rome, 1924) 1-18.

¹⁵⁹ S. Breton, *Mystique de la Passion* (Tournai, 1962) epecially chap. 3, 49-70.

¹⁶⁰ See art. "Alphonse de Ligouri (saint)," DS, vol. 1, cols. 357-389.

¹⁶¹ St. Alphonsus, *The Practice of the Love of Jesus Christ* in *The Way of St. Alphonsus Ligouri*, ed. by B. Ulanov (New York, 1960) 132-200.

¹⁶² See art. "France," DS, vol. 5, col. 969.

¹⁶³ See art. "Foucauld (Charles de)," DS, vol. 5, cols. 729-741.

¹⁶⁴ See art. "Huvelin (Henri)," DS, vol. 7, cols. 1200-1204.

¹⁶⁵ M. Carrouges, *Soldier of the Spirit. Life of Charles de Foucauld* (New York, 1956) 87.

¹⁶⁶ Charles de Foucauld, *Lettres á Henry de Castries* (Paris 1938) 97.

¹⁶⁷ Charles de Foucauld, letter to Mme de Bondy in *Oeuvres spirituelles, Anthologie* (Paris, 1958) 30.

¹⁶⁸ April 26, 1900, *ibid.*, 35.

¹⁶⁹ R. Voillaume, "The Mystery of Nazareth," in *Seeds of the Desert. The Legacy of Charles de Foucauld* (Chicago, 1955) 51-69.

¹⁷⁰ J.-F. Six, *The Spiritual Autobiography of Charles de Foucauld* (New York, 1964). See section on "Life of Jesus," 79-103.

¹⁷¹ Retreat of 1904; see Charles de Foucauld, *Oeuvres spirituelles, Anthologie* (Paris, 1958) 555.

[172] April, 1914 in S. Chauleur, *Charles de Foucauld et Mère Saint-Michel, abbesse des clarisses de Nazareth;* see also his letters on May 13, 1903 and May 6, 1912, *ibid.,* 44, 57.

[173] Letter to Mère Saint-Michel, November 13, 1905, *ibid.,* 44.

[174] H. Monier Vinard, "La spiritualité du P. de Foucauld," RAM 9 (1928) 408.

NOTES TO CHAPTER 3

[1] G. Tarde, *Les Lois de l'imitation* (Paris, 1890) and *La logique sociale* (Paris, 1895).

[2] A. Burloud, *Psychologie* (Paris, 1948) 106.

[3] P. Guillaume, *Manuel de psychologie,* 7th ed. (Paris, 1952) 60.

[4] Max Scheler, "Vorbilder und Fuhrer," in *Schriften aus dem Nachlass,* vol. 1 (Berlin, 1933); FT: *Le saint, le genie, le heros* (Lyons and Paris, 1958) 27.

[5] *Ibid.,* 28.

[6] Henri Bergson, *Two Sources of Morality and Religion* (New York, 1935) 26.

[7] G. Gusdorf, *Traité de l'existence morale* (Paris, 1949) 158-159, 161.

[8] E. Barbotin, *Le témoignage spirituel* (Paris, 1964) 145-146.

[9] See the article "États de vie," DS, vol. 4, cols. 1406-1428 and in the present series the volume *A Christian Anthropology.*

[10] See in the present series the volume *Jesus in Christian Devotion and Contemplation.*

[11] Francis de Sales, *Introduction to the Devout Life,* 2nd part, chap. 1 (New York, 1949) 40.

[12] Pierre de Bérulle, *Oeuvres de Piété,* no. 54 (77) (Paris, 1944) 202.

[13] Pierre de Bérulle, *Correspondance,* vol. 3, no. 541, ed. J. Dagens (Pais and Louvain, 1939) 58.

[14] C. Marmion, *Christ in His Mysteries* (St. Louis, 1939) 25-26.

[15] V. Lossky, *The Mytical Theology of the Eastern Church* (London, 1957) 215.

[16] A. Tanquerey, *The Spiritual Life,* no. 961 (Westminster, Md., 1930) 454.

[17] See, for example, B. Häring, *The Law of Christ* (Westminster, Md., 1963).

[18] B. Häring, *Le sacré et le bien* (Paris, 1963), chap. 5, "Morale de l'imitation," 263.

[19] Augustine, *Holy Virginity,* FC 27, 174.

NOTES TO CHAPTER 4

[1] P. Blanc, *Guy Michard* (Toulouse, 1948) 55.

² See also art. "Jésus-Christ," DS, which will be translated in the present series.

³ "Imitation did not make sons, but filiation made imitators," in M. Luther, *Werke*, vol. 2 (Weimar, 1884) 518.

⁴ G. Salet, *La vie pour moi, c'est le Christ* (Le Puy, 1941) 22-23.

⁵ Ignatius of Loyola, *Spiritual Exercises*, no. 104.

⁶ John XXIII, *Humanae salutis*, bull of convocation of Vatican Council II, Dec. 25, 1961, in *The Documents of Vatican II* (New York, 1966) 703-706.

NOTES TO CHAPTER 5

¹ All quotations from the references to the *Imitation of Christ* are to edition of Ronald Knox and Michael Oakley, New York, Sheed and Ward, 1959.

² See DS, vol. 3, cols. 727-735. A *rapiarium* is a literary composition consisting of quotations from various spiritual writers.

³ See DS, vol. 5, cols. 430-431.

⁴ See DS, vol. 6, cols. 1169-1175.

⁵ See P. Debongnie, "Les thèmes de l'Imitation," *Revue de'histoire ecclésiastique* 36 (1940) 327-328.

⁶ *Ibid.*, 335.

⁷ See Vatican II, *Constitution on the Sacred Liturgy*, preface, no. 2.

BIBLIOGRAPHY

Chapter 1

Primary Sources

Augustine, *Holy Virginity*, FC 27.

Epictetus, *Discourses*. Loeb Classical Library, vol. 1. Cambridge: 1956, 308-309.

Mekiltha, ed. and trans. J. Z. Lauterbach. Philadelphia: 1935.

Testaments of the Twelve Patriarchs in *The Apocrpha and Pseudepigrapha of the Old Testament*, 2 vols., ed. R. H. Charles, vol. 2. Oxford: 1913, 296-360.

Secondary Sources

Abrahams, I., *Studies in Pharasaism and the Gospels*, vol. 2. Cambridge: 1924, 138-182.

Boer, W. P. de, *The Imitation of Paul*. Kampen: 1962.

Cerfaux, L., *The Christian in the Theology of St. Paul*. New York: 1967.

Cullmann, Oscar, *The Christology of the New Testament*. Philadelphia: 1959.

Davies, W. D., *The Setting of the Sermon on the Mount*. Cambridge: 1964.

Dibelius, M., *From Tradition to Gospel*. New York: no date.

Dodd, C. H., *"Ennomos Christou,"* in *Studia Paulina in honorem J. de Zwaan*. Haarlem: 1953, 96-110.

————, *Historical Tradition in the Fourth Gospel*. Cambridge: 1963.

————,"A Hidden Parable in the 4th Gospel," in *More New Testament Studies*. Grand Rapids: 1968, 30-40.

Fraine, J. de. *Adam and the Family of Man*. New York: 1965.

Gerhardsson, B., *Memory and Manuscript. Oral Tradition and Written Transmission in Rabbinic Judaism and Early Christianity*. Upsala: 1961.

Goetz, J., et al., *A Christian Anthropology*, RES. Saint Meinrad, Indiana: 1974.

Guitton, J., *The Problem of Jesus*. New York: 1955.

Gundry, R. H., " 'Verba Christi' in 1 Peter: Their Implications Concerning the Authorship of 1 Peter and the Authenticity of the Gospel Tradition," *New Testament Studies* 13 (1967) 336-350.

Gwyn Griffiths, J., "The Disciple's Cross," *New Testament Studies* 16 (1970) 358-364.

Jeremias, J., *"Pais theou,"* in TDNT, vol. 5, 677-717.

Kittel, G., *"Akoloutheō,"* in TDNT, vol. 1, 210-216.

Martin, R. P., *Phil 2:5-11 iin Recent Interpretation and in the Setting of Early Christian Worship*. Cambridge: 1967.

Michaelis, W., *"Mimeomai, etc.,"* in TDNT, vol. 4, 659-674.

Plummer, A., *The Second Epistle of St. Paul to the Corinthians*. International Critical Commentary. New York: 1915.

Proudfoot, C. M., "Imitation or Realistic Participation? A Study of Paul's Concept of 'Suffering with Christ'," *Interpretation* 17 (1963) 140-160.

Ratzinger, J., *Introduction to Christianity*. New York: 1970.

Rengstorf, K. H., *Manthanō*, in TDNT, vol. 4, 291-413.

Schnackenberg, R., *The Moral Teaching of the New Testament*. Freiburg: 1965.

Spicq, C. *Agape in the New Testament*, vol. 3. St. Louis: 1966.

Stanley, David, " 'Become Imitators of Me': the Pauline Conception of Apostolic Tradition," *Biblica* 40 (1959) 859-877.

————, "Paul and the Christian Concept of the Servant of God," in *The Apostolic Church in the New Testament*. Westminster, Md.: 1965, 312-351.

Tinsley, E. J., *The Imitation of God in Christ. An Essay on the Biblical Basis of Christian Spirituality*. London: 1960.

Chapter 2

Primary Sources

Augustine, *The Christian Combat* in *Writings of St. Augustine: Christian Instruction. Admonition and Grace. The Christian Combat. Faith, Hope and Charity*, FC 2.

————, *The Trinity* FC 45.

Bernard, *Concerning Grace and Free Will*. New York: 1920.

————, *On the Love of God*. Trappist, Kentucky: 1943.

————, *On the Song of Songs*. 2 vols. Dublin: 1920.

————, *On the Song of Songs*, CF 4.

————, *St. Bernard's Sermons for the Seasons and the Principal Festivals of the Year*. Westminster, Md.: 1950.

————, *The Steps of Humility*, Cambridge, Mass.: 1950.

Cyprian, *Book on the Value of Patience* in *Treatises*, FC 36.

————, *Exhortation to Martyrdom, to Fortunatus* in *Treatises*, FC 36.

The Didache. The Epistle of Barnabas. The Epistles and Martyrdom of St. Polycarp. The Fragments of Papias. The Epistle to Diognetus, ACW 6.

Early Franciscan Classics. New Jersey: 1962.

The Epistles of St. Clement of Rome and St. Ignatius of Antioch, ACW 1.

Eusebius, *Ecclesiastical History*, FC 19 and 29.

Ignatius of Loyola, *The Spiritual Exercises*, ed. Louis J. Puhl. Chicago: 1951.

Irenaeus, *Against Heresies*, ANF, vol. 1.

John Chrysostom, *Baptismal Instruction*, ACW 31.

————, *Commentary on Galatians*, NPNF, 1st ser., vol. 13.

————, *Homilies on the Acts*, NPNF, 1st ser., vol. 11.

————, *Homilies on 1 Corinthians*, NPNF, 1st ser., vol. 12.

————, *Homilies on Ephesians*, NPNF, 1st ser., vol. 13.

————, *Homilies on the Gospel of St. Matthew*, NPNF, 1st ser., vol. 10.

————, *Homilies on Philippians*, NPNF, 1st ser., vol. 13.

————, *Homilies on Romans*, NPNF, 1st ser., vol. 11.

————, *Homilies on St. John's Gospel*, FC 33 and 41.

Leo the Great, *Sermons*, NPNF, 2nd ser., vol. 12.

Origen, *Exhortation to Martyrdom*, ACW 19.

Saint Francis of Assisi. New York: 1959.

St. Francis of Assisi, *The Legends and Lauds*. New York: 1948.

The Spiritual Doctrine of Father Louis Lallemant. Westminster, Md.: 1946.

The Legend and Writings of St. Clare of Assisi. Saint Bonaventure, New York: 1953.

Thomas Aquinas, *Commentary on Ephesians*. Albany, New York: 1966.

The Way of St. Alphonsus Ligouri, ed. B. Ulanov. New York: 1960.

The Works of Bonaventure, ed. J. Guy Bougerol. New Jersey: 1964.

Secondary Sources

Bouyer, L., *The Spirituality of the New Testament and the Fathers*. New York: 1963.

Carrouges, M., *Soldier of the Spirit. Life of Charles de Foucauld*. New York: 1956.

Humel, E. L., *The Concept of Martyrdom according to St. Cyprian*. Washington: 1946.

Mersch, E., *The Whole Christ*. Milwaukee: 1938.

Noye, I. et al, *Jesus in Christian Devotion and Contemplation*, RES. Saint Meinrad, Indiana: 1974.

Ohleyer, L. J., *The Pauline Formula "induere Christum" with Special Reference to the Works of St. John Chrysostom*. Washington: 1921.

Pourrat, P., *Christian Spirituality*, vol. 3. Westminster, Md.: 1953.

Six, J.-F., *The Spiritual Autobiography of Charles de Foucauld*. New York: 1964.

Tinsley, E. J., "*The Imitatio Christi* in the Mysticism of St. Ignatius . . ." *Studia patristica*, Texte und Untersuchungen vol. 2. Berlin: 1955, 553-560.

Voillaume, R., "The Mystery of Nazareth," in *Seeds of the Desert. The Legacy of Charles de Foucauld*. Chicago: 1955.

Chapter 3

Primary Sources

Augustine, *Holy Virginity*, FC 27.

Bergson, H., *Two Sources of Morality and Religion*. New York: 1935.

Francis de Sales, *Introduction to the Devout Life*. New York: 1949.

Secondary Sources

Häring, B., *The Law of Christ*. Westminster, Md.: 1963.

Lossky, V., *The Mystical Theology of the Eastern Church*. London: 1957.

Marmion, C., *Christ in His Mysteries*. St. Louis: 1939.

Tanquerey, A., *The Spiritual Life*. Westminster, Md.: 1930.

Chapter 4

Primary Sources

Ignatius of Loyola, *The Spiritual Exercises*. Ed. Louis J. Puhl.

Chicago: 1951.

Secondary Sources

Grandmaison, L. de, *Jesus Christ*. New York: 1938.

Guibert, J. de, *Theology of the Spiritual Life*. New York: 1953.

John XXIII, *Humanae salutis* in *The Documents of Vatican II*. New York: 1966.

Lebreton, J., *The Spiritual Teaching of the New Testament*. Westminster, Md.: 1960.

Marmion, C., *Christ in His Mysteries*. St. Louis: 1939.

———, *Christ the Ideal of the Monk*. St. Louis: 1926.

———, *Christ the Life of the Soul*. St. Louis: 1935.

Mouroux, J., *The Christian Expereince*. New York: 1954.

Ramsay, A. Michael, *God, Christ and the World*. London: 1969.

Stolz, A., *The Doctrine of Spiritual Direction*. London: 1946.

Chapter 5

Primary Sources

Constitution on the Sacred Liturgy in *The Documents of Vatican II*. New York: 1966.

Imitation of Christ. Ed. Ronald Knox and Michael Oakley. New York: 1959.